SODA POP.

SODA POP.

The History, Advertising, Art and Memorabilia of Soft Drinks in America.

Lawrence Dietz

Simon and Schuster

A Subsistence Press Book

Published by arrangement with
Chelsea House Publishers

TO
MARK AND NATALIE DIETZ
AND LEAH SCHAEFER

Because the collection of the artifacts of Coca-Cola and other brands of soda pop is a passion which has managed to elude a fair number of people, and because certain serious types have insisted on viewing that passion solely as an exercise in sociology. I think that I should confess that the genesis of this book came in a junk shop on Mc-Allister Street in San Francisco in 1965.

I was up from Los Angeles visiting friends, and we were spending a day looking for a rocking chair for their house. As they haggled over prices in a store, I noticed two serving trays for Coke (the 1927 soda jerk and the 1929 bathing girl, to be exact) sitting in a pile of junk. I was 25, and I had never consciously noticed a Coke tray before that moment. I wish that I could report that I immediately saw those trays as some sort of metaphor for, or symbol of, America! America! But, in fact, all they were, was beautiful, and I asked the owner how much he was asking for them. Fifty cents each, he said.

In the only decent bargaining I have ever managed with a dealer in second-hand goods, I told him that I had only fifty cents on me, and asked him if he'd take that. He did. I took the trays back to L.A. and put them up on a wall.

A couple of weeks later, I was driving around and saw

in the window of a flossy shop on the Sunset Strip a set of four Hires Root Beer trays (all, I was later to learn, from the years 1914–1917), priced at $12.50 each. My first reaction was incredulity. How could any store owner, even one catering to the wealthy, try and pass a fifty-cent bit of goods as being worth $12.50?

During this period, I was a free-lance magazine writer, a state of existence resembling chronic unemployment. I was spending a large portion of my free time prowling the L.A. area—driving down streets for mile-after-mile-after-mile just for the hell of it—and I began to suspect that I had been exceedingly lucky in buying my Coke trays for such a low price. For one thing, the Hires trays quickly disappeared from that shop; for another, I began to run across a number of shops which specialized in selling strange stuff—World War II posters, old beer signs, 1930s' movie posters, old railroad schedules; in short, all of the promotional ephemera which corporations and the government have spewed out over the years. Most of it was expensive, or at least, relatively expensive if you started asking yourself why someone would lay out $2.50 for a 1919 grocery store price list.

I was finally confronted by my growing seriousness of interest in all this stuff when I happened to wander into a shop called The Green Door in Long Beach. The proprietors, Mr. and Mrs. Pryor, who looked as if they had been drawn by Norman Rockwell, had gathered together an astonishing variety of material—from suffragette tracts to coin-operated music machines from the turn of the century; and of course, memorabilia of Coca-Cola.

Specifically, there were two trays which riveted my attention: a 1904 Lillian Nordica; and a 1908 tray, put out by the Western Coca-Cola Bottling Company of Chicago without authorization from the people in Atlanta, which showed a half-nude woman clutching a bottle of Coke. They were asking $47.50 for the Nordica tray, and the "naked lady" tray simply wasn't for sale—Mrs. Pryor liked having it around.

After a lot of self-imposed *angst,* I shelled out something like seventy bucks for the Nordica tray and two others. Over the next few months, I kept dropping in and establishing my claim against the day when Mrs. Pryor would give up the rare nude tray. One day she did.

I wound up feverishly buying advertising materials put out for Coca-Cola, with occasional forays into Pepsi, 7-Up, Nehi, Hires, Moxie, Nu-Grape, Dr. Pepper, and Orange Crush. Perhaps I *was* a little strange, but then, I figured, the people who were paying thousands of dollars for paintings of American flags and silk-screens of soup cans were stone nuts.

My mania paid off when the art director of the Los Angeles *Times* Sunday Magazine, *West,* sold his superiors on the idea of a giant story on Coca-Cola, which I would write and which would be illustrated by examples of Coca-Cola advertising. We soon learned that the Coca-Cola Company maintains archives, so the art director and I went down to do some research. Archives! I felt as though I were making a religious pilgrimage.

The first day we had lunch with some Coca-Cola Company executives. I had gotten up late and had only a cup of coffee before I rushed to the restaurant. We ordered drinks, and I immediately got giddy. (Ordinarily, when I go to a business lunch without having had breakfast, I order a Coke if other people are drinking. In Atlanta, I thought that this would make the men from Coca-Cola think I was playing up to them; somehow, it seemed important to maintain the illusion of journalistic distance.)

The conversation drifted to the proposition that there should be a museum in Atlanta for memorabilia of Coca-Cola, Coca-Cola being at least as important to Atlanta as the Civil War. One of the executives mentioned something about plans for exhibits to be displayed in the new Company headquarters building. In my sodden state, I took that to mean that the Company was *planning* a new building, so I lurched into a brilliant exposition of the idea that the new building be built in the shape of a giant Coca-Cola bottle, all green glass and fifteen stories high. While I was laboriously explaining that the air-conditioning equipment could be hidden in the metal "bottle cap," I glanced up, only to see three somber faces staring down at the table. I'll never know whether they thought I was making fun of their product or taking it too seriously.

Over the next few days, as we ferreted through various files and a warehouse filled with old advertising materials (the Kaaba), I began to find that however proud some executives are of the Company's advertising, contemplation of its history makes some of them uneasy. For one thing, looking to the past is equated with that dark period when Pepsi was merchandised as the drink of "now" sophisticates ("For those who think young"). For another, the triumph of Coca-Cola advertising in establishing its vision of America has led it to be symbolic of the country—not a bad thing until foreigners began to talk about "Coca-colonization" (speaking not about Coca-Cola, but about America), and dissident Americans began to view Coke as an Establishment elixir.

I also found that Coca-Cola advertising, like pure art, did not readily lend itself to verbalization. Anyone who has ever felt acutely uncomfortable with art critics' jargon ("There is clarity of color here as if in contradiction to the mysteries of theme and pattern") may have deduced that it is difficult for an outsider to adequately describe visual inspiration.

While advertising for Coke was created in far different circumstances than pure art, none of it seemed to have been produced to a specific and irrevocable order, such as, "Paint me a soda jerk leaning forward with a glass of Coke in his hand." Instead, Coca-Cola advertising has always aspired to convey a set of visions of America; in addition, for much of the Company's history, the ads had not only to upstage the advertising of competitors, but also to counter the effects of a series of bum raps with which the government was trying to hang the Company.

I mixed the history of the Company with a history of its advertising; the piece ran, and I was deluged with reader mail. People, it seemed, were curious about the history of the drink they had been so enthusiastically drinking. There was another flood of mail after the *Times* put the piece on its wire service, and it was picked up by a few dozen newspapers around the country and the world. The letters convinced me that there were a lot of people interested in soda pop, so I began sending letters to book publishers, some of whom were amused and frosty, most of whom were unamused and frosty.

Finally, of course, I got a contract and I went back to Atlanta. I promptly contracted walking pneumonia, but I dug around for any stuff I missed on the first go-round. Then I went to St. Louis, the headquarters for the D'Arcy Advertising Agency, which had served Coca-Cola from 1906 to 1956. I hoped, of course, to find incredibly detailed memos that would lay out the secret of Coca-Cola advertising. Naturally enough, all of the files on Coca-Cola had mouldered for a few years after the agency had lost the account, and then during a move, been thrown out.

I did find a few packets of stuff, but more importantly, I got to talk to Henry Heier and Art Praechter, who were both artists at D'Arcy and who worked on the Coke account during the 1940s. However difficult it is for an outsider to talk about art, it is equally so for the creator. ("How would you describe the creation of your *Sunflowers,* Mr. Van Gogh?" "To start with, I used mostly yellow.") Heier is the guy who created the famous Coca-Cola "Sprite," that mysterious creature who wore a bottle cap for a hat; but all he rem-members about the specifics for the creation was that he was to come up with a symbolic creature to represent Coke, one that was "neither male nor female." So he sat down and painted one—an exquisitely detailed bit of work for what was supposed to be a rough comp, which was approved and then shipped to Chicago where another artist, Haddon Sundbloom, did a finished rendition.

My fantasy, of course, was that guys like Heier and Praechter spent a lot of their time prowling around, visiting soda fountains and the like, so that they could rush back to their drawing boards and get it all down. It didn't happen that way. It all came out of their heads and the imagination of D'Arcy's Archie Lee, the genius who headed the Coca-Cola account. Lee died in 1950, so I went to lunch with his son, and then went home to L.A.

It may seem astonishing that a simple, cheap, non-essential drink should have become symbolic of a country and its mores. It is perhaps somewhat less astonishing when you consider the fact that since the drink was invented in 1886, The Coca-Cola Company has spent over $700,000,000 in advertising Coke. Based on that figure, I would estimate that the entire soft-drink industry has spent about $1 billion in advertising during that period.

This, then, is the story of soda pop and its advertising. If this book appears to be the story of Coca-Cola, the reason is obvious: Coca-Cola is to the soft drink business what Steinway is to pianos or Bayer is to aspirin—only more so.

CHAPTER 1

In the beginning, there was Globe of Flower Cough Syrup, Indian Queen Hair Dye, Triplex Liver Pills, Gingerine, and a blood medicine called Extract of Styllinger. All of these patent medicines were cooked up in the twenty years following the Civil War by an obscure Georgia pharmacist named John S. Pemberton. Pemberton was no quack; he lived in an age of pharmacological entrepreneurism, when the corner druggist knew as much as the researchers for national drug manufacturers. What's more, the local druggist *knew* that he knew as much, and since he himself could produce a nostrum as effective (and with as high an alcoholic content) as any nationally-marketed drug, he saw no reason not to do so. Besides, the profit margin was greater. Thus Pemberton, like almost everyone else in his profession, kept working with the kettles and test tubes in his lab to create potions that would make people feel better.

Sometime after moving his business from Columbus, Georgia (where he was a practicing pharmaceutical chemist, as well as the operator of a retail outlet known for the wide range of its soda fountain concoctions) to Atlanta (where he was primarily a manufacturer), Pemberton finally perfected an innocuous mixture of extract of kola nut, fruit syrup, and extract of coca leaf. There is no clear record of what medical results, if any, Pemberton expected of his new creation. Since it wasn't as obviously potent as an alcoholic medicine (alcohol being the essential ingredient in patent medicines) and since it tasted good, it might be assumed that he saw it as a simple pick-me-up.

Civic pride being what it is, there are people around Columbus who will swear that Pemberton was dispensing drinks made from this syrup as early as 1867, when he still operated the apothecary shop in Columbus. Most accounts, however, point to a day in May of 1886, when Pemberton took a quantity of his syrup to Jacobs' Drug Store in Atlanta, where he asked the fountain man to mix some up. This done, everyone had a taste, and the fount man agreed to dispense the beverage on a trial basis.

The next thing Pemberton had to do was get a name for his new syrup. His previous efforts had proved him something less than an ace in brand-naming. Luckily, this time he had three partners in his business. All four dreamed up names and voted among them. Frank Robinson, the bookkeeper, suggested the catchy "Coca-Cola," which was unanimously adopted.

Whereupon Coca-Cola almost sank without a bubble, since Pemberton originally envisioned mixing the syrup with ice and plain water; and we all know how inspiring a flat soft drink is. The mixing of the syrup with carbonated water was an accident, probably on the part of the fount man at Jacobs', but even this fortuitous circumstance did not ensure the immediate success of the drink. Although Pemberton invested the grand sum of $73.96 in advertising his product—the only record of this expenditure is the memory of several oil-cloth banners, which were hung outside soda fountains in Atlanta—he sold only 25 gallons of syrup, at $1 the gallon, during the first year of the drink's existence.

If the ratio of advertising expense to gross sales wasn't sobering enough, Pemberton's health began to fail. We can judge his faith in his own remedies by the fact that he treated his physical decline by getting rid of the heartache of his business: no Extract of Styllinger for old John. He sold out piecemeal, and he sold out cheap—two-thirds of the business going for $1200, and the last third being disposed of from his deathbed for $550.

The particulars of the sale of the first piece of the business have provided for a great deal of good Georgia gossip.

Since the first chunk of the company changed hands several times over the next few years, hundreds of Georgians have since claimed that their family either had possession of, or a shot at, control of Coca-Cola.

The man who did wind up with the controlling interest — at one point the entire physical assets of the Coca-Cola part of Pemberton's business were delivered to him in a one-horse wagon — was a 37-year-old Atlanta wholesale druggist named Asa Candler. Although it took Candler until 1891 to acquire the last third of the business, between 1889 and 1890 he began to merchandise aggressively the only valuable part of Pemberton's property: Coca-Cola.

Ironically, Candler did not immediately recognize the value of one of the greatest assets of Coca-Cola. Frank Robinson (who had followed the Company after the sale, and who would be bookkeeper, as well as an officer of the Coca-Cola Company after its formal organization in 1891), who had created the name Coca-Cola, had also written it out in an exaggerated Spencerian script. Although this would turn out to be the single most valuable piece of commercial calligraphy ever produced in the world, it was considered so unremarkable at the time that it was not used on an 1891 calendar, which Candler had printed up to advertise Coca-Cola (and one of his other products, a tooth whitener called De-Lec-Ta-Lave [page 34]:)

Despite this immediate oversight, sales of Coca-Cola began to increase (from 1,049 gallons of syrup in 1887 to 2,171 in 1889) as soon as Candler acquired his first interest in the drink. He had given a job to a nephew named Sam Dobbs, who urged a promotional and advertising blitz for Coca-Cola. As Candler took that advice, sales soared: 8,855 gallons in 1890; 19,831 in 1891; and 35,360 gallons the year after that.

Candler's immediate vision of the use of Coca-Cola, however, was not far removed from Pemberton's, and so the early advertising was medicinal in tone, a fact that has embarrassed the Company ever since. In 1890, for example, Candler distributed copies of *Grier's Almanac* to advertise products sold by his wholesale drug firm. The front cover promoted De-Lec-Ta-Lave, Howard's Hair Dye, and Old Doctor Lindsey Durham's Woman Cure, while the back cover trumpeted the virtues of Bradfield's Female Regulator.

Inside, amidst the ads for Dr. Cheney's Expectorant ("Stop that cough"), Botanic Blood Balm ("Cures scrofula, kidney troubles, catarrh"), and Dr. Moffett's Indian Weed Female Medicine ("A sure friend"), was a full page which proclaimed the glories of a "Wonderful Nerve and Brain Tonic and Remarkable Therapeutic Agent." You guessed it. That was Coca-Cola, which was also described as "Delightful! Refreshing! Stimulating! Invigorating!"

Like most other medicinal ads of the period, this one contained testimonials. Doctor C. A. Stiles of Atlanta proclaimed: "Have almost invariably obtained favorable results from Coca-Cola in insomnia, neuralgia, periodical sick headache, and in those troubles arising from biliousness, indigestion, and mental exhaustion; also in dyspnoea due to laryngeal reflexes, and in those cases where the voice has been inordinately excited by singing and speaking." Anyone comparison-shopping for medical service might have been more impressed with Dr. Robert W. Westmoreland of Atlanta, who wrote: "From a knowledge of the medicinal agents comprising the formula of Coca-Cola, together with a personal experience of its effects, I feel safe in recommending the preparation as an agreeable tonic, a pleasant and refreshing beverage, while its efficacy as a remedy for nervous headache will commend it to those suffering from that malady." Anyone who didn't trust doctors could find comfort in the words of an employee of the State Library of Georgia, who wrote, "Gentlemen: It affords me pleasure to state that in my opinion, after a faithful trial of it, the Coca-Cola is all that is claimed for it. In cases of mental and physical exhaustion from over-work it is the best tonic I have ever tried. It is an almost certain cure for headache arising from nervous depression, or overexcitement, and I believe it to be good for indigestion. Yours very respectfully, Jno. Milledge."

Anyone who could resist two doctors and one librarian was induced to try the drink by a simple expedient: Candler gave it away. Thousands of coupons were distributed, redeemable at local drugstores for free glasses of Coke. Used coupons were sent back to the Company by the druggists, who were then reimbursed for the full retail value of the Coke they had given away.

In 1893, with sales of 48,427 gallons of syrup, the Company spent $12,000 in advertising. That's 12 percent of sales, which, considering Coke was a new product, is not a high figure. (In 1966, when Coca-Cola Company sales were $979 million, *Advertising Age* estimated that the Company spent $71 million in advertising in the United States.)

The advertising of this period, done by lithographers like Wolf & Company of Philadelphia, is distinguished today only for its rarity. The standard scene showed a woman holding a fountain glass of Coke. Somewhere in the scene, straining to appear natural, would be a sign with the logo for Coca-Cola. The one stylistic trick in each ad was in having something on a counter—either another trade card or a free drink coupon or an envelope and letter—which had some miniscule writing on it concerning Coke. Those patient enough to make out what was written there often were rewarded with nothing more than a list of the branch offices of the Company. To look at it more positively, anyone suffering eyestrain was likely to drink another Coca-Cola.

By then, Candler was ignoring the middle-man technique of getting his medical claims from the testimonials of doctors. The front side of a trade card of the period shows a woman holding a glass of Coke at a soda fountain; the back, all text, reads: "Coca-Cola is not simply a nicely flavored syrup, but contains, in a remarkable degree, the tonic properties of the wonderful Erythroxylon Coca Plant of South America, which has a worldwide reputation for sustaining the vital power under conditions of extraordinary fatigue, and affords prompt relief for mental and physical exhaustion, or nervous prostration. It also has the stimulating, enlivening, reviving properties of the extract from the celebrated African Cola nut. This forms the choicest, most desirable and efficacious remedial combination possible.

"Coca-Cola renews the vigor of the intellect, rendering the flow of thought more easy and the reasoning power more vigorous; it conduces to mental clearness and activity, freedom from fatigue and power of endurance.

"It has gained an enviable reputation, and has taken position at the very front of the leading and popular soda fountain beverages.

"Coca-Cola is making large and rapid strides in all directions, reaching out into new fields and acquiring great popularity where it had before been unknown. Its reputation has been fully established everywhere as a remarkable seller, summer and winter, North and South.

"We have the facts and figures to show that millions are using Coca-Cola, and while we cannot produce their individual testimony, the only logical conclusion is that they drink it for the beneficial and agreeable results obtained.

"Its immediate and beneficial effects upon the diseases of the vocal chords are wonderful. By its use the husky voice can be made clear and natural, and all other affections of the throat can be relieved. In periodical sickness and the headache consequent upon it, its effect is marvelous, strengthening the system and relieving it of all impurities."

It is axiomatic that drama in the theater consists of getting the protagonist up a tree and then getting him down again in time for the curtain. Candler appeared to have tied Coca-Cola to the upper-most leaves of the "wonderful Erythroxylon Coca Plant," a position which, if kept, would probably have given Coca-Cola a market life only slightly longer than Dr. Moffett's Indian Weed. But Candler brilliantly reversed his field and began to market his drink, not as a medicinal balm with specific curing properties, but rather as a leisure refreshment for the masses.

POP.

CHAPTER 2

In America today, when the concept of leisure-time enjoyment is as dear as sex and as near as television, the idea of a non-alcoholic 5¢ beverage being hot stuff in leisure-time enjoyment as well as the cutting edge of an earthshaking sociological change, is absolutely quaint. In 1900 however, only the rich enjoyed themselves. The middle class and the poor, unorganized working class were living out what sociologist Max Weber has called the Protestant Ethic—the idea that man's salvation in the hereafter came through hard, joyless work in the here and now. Operating under this theory, the worker who died of TB in a sweatshop after working twelve-hour days, six days a week, for fifty cents a day, died at least with the somewhat dubious consolation that he or she was going to heaven.

There were, of course, *divertissements* for the working man: in the cities, for example, local political machines sponsored outings or picnics. But these were planned events, occasional respites from a bleak and generally despairing life. To be able to choose, spontaneously, one's own moment of leisure enjoyment was simply not part of American life (though the then-nascent labor unions were working toward this goal, among others). Yet Candler and Dobbs decided to market Coca-Cola as such a pastime.

There is no record of the deliberations which led up

23.

to Candler's and Dobbs' decision. They may have come to the reali-
zation that the sale of Coca-Cola depended almost exclusively on the
number of people near a drugstore or soda fountain who felt lousy.
Since it might be assumed that most people felt fairly good most of
the time, it stood to reason that most of the time they would have no
call to drink Coca-Cola. Simple pragmatism suggests broadening
out the market. But there was also the question of social responsibility.

Candler would have had to be blind not to see that
Americans were seriously concerned by the dangers of long-term
use of patent medicines and opiates. This public outcry would finally
result in the passage of the Pure Food and Drug Act in 1906, and of
various statutes limiting the use of opiates (which had been rather
easily available both through doctors and druggists). But Candler
was not one to wait for legislation; he knew that Coca-Cola would
be a villain if he waited to act.

Aside from the specific promises made in his advertising, there was the matter of the actual content of Coca-Cola.
Pemberton's original formula used untreated "Erythroxylon Coca
plants," and the untreated plant contains, on each leaf, a minute
amount of cocaine. In retrospect, it is easy to understand why Pemberton did not choose to treat the small amount of leaf used in the
formula so as to remove the even smaller amount of cocaine in the
drink. For one thing, the amount in a drink was miniscular; for another, such eminent doctors of the period as Sigmund Freud were
openly prescribing the drug for their patients. Why bother, then, to
remove something that was under no suspicion? But Candler found
himself operating the business during the period when the effect of
much larger doses of the drug was becoming known. That was bad
enough, but worse still, he was put in the embarrassing position of
having to admit openly that the drink contained the drug. Around
1900, in an effort to defend the purity of the component elements
of Coca-Cola, Candler solicited an analysis of the drink by a research
chemist, whose findings were reproduced by the Company in a booklet titled *What Is It? What It Is.* The chemist reported that there was
a "trace" of cocaine in the drink, such a small trace that someone
bent on getting a kick would have had to guzzle over five-and-one-
half quarts of Coca-Cola, at one sitting, to even begin to feel the

24.

effects of the drug. (Anyone drinking five-and-one-half quarts of *anything* at one sitting is bound to feel the effects.) Candler immediately ordered the Company chemists to treat the coca leaf used in the formula, and by 1905, no Coca-Cola was produced which contained even the trace amount of the drug.*

It is a matter of historical record that most American industries, when publicly confronted by the charges of wrongdoing, from pollution to dangerous working conditions and exploitation of workers, follow a shabby script which includes intransigence, violence, political maneuvering and/or vote-buying, and bitter grumbling (both before and after any changes made to comply with public opinion or legislation). This scenario has been less the style of The Coca-Cola Company than practically any other major American corporation, stemming, perhaps, from the example Candler set in the late 1890s.

Strangely enough, the greatest difficulty Candler was to have over an ingredient of Coca-Cola was with caffeine. The chemist reporting in Candler's booklet had allowed that Coca-Cola did contain caffeine, but said that caffeine was relatively harmless, and appeared in the drink in very small amounts. (Four six-ounce drinks of Coca-Cola contain less caffeine than one five-ounce cup of coffee.) Even so, through the mid-1920s there was steady criticism of the caffeine in Coke, so much so that the Company felt impelled to issue, in 1923, another booklet defending the product. Among flowery tributes to the purity and quality of Coca-Cola, there was a spirited defense of caffeine and a favorable comparison of the amounts contained in equal portions of Coca-Cola, tea, and coffee.

Even as Candler was opening a potentially wider market for Coca-Cola by physically and metaphysically separating it from the drug section of the drugstore, a 28-year-old man operating a retail confectionery business in Vickburg, Mississippi was—quite without the knowledge or approval of the men in Atlanta—experi-

---

* There the matter rested until the late 1960s, when the rise of the "drug culture" in the United States prompted crackpot rumors that the drink still contained the drug. Preposterous though the rumors were, they gained some small currency, because the formula for Coca-Cola remains a secret, and in the minds of some of the drug crowd, secrecy is, by definition, an admission of guilt.

menting with a radical new method of widening the distribution of Coca-Cola.

Joseph Biedenharn had been selling Coca-Cola since 1890, when Sam Dobbs brought a keg of Coca-Cola syrup into Biedenharn's store and explained what it was. Biedenharn, after being assured that no other ingredients save carbonated water were needed, agreed to try and sell the drink. Sell it he did, and about a year later Asa Candler himself paid a call on Biedenharn.

Candler wanted Biedenharn to act as a jobber for Coca-Cola in the area around Vicksburg, the agreement being that Biedenharn would buy 2,000 gallons of syrup during the following twelve months, subject to a 25¢-per-gallon rebate at the end of that period. It was a profitable arrangement for both parties, since Biedenharn sold more syrup than the minimum amount specified in the agreement. Coincident to Candler's first visit, Biedenharn was visited by some customers who came in with confectionery orders for parties to be thrown over the Fourth of July for plantation field hands. The customers also wanted ten cases of bottled soda water apiece, so Biedenharn telephoned the soda water plant in Vicksburg to obtain the thirty cases. The manager refused to sell that much soda water, claiming that he needed it for his own customers.

It was a fateful moment: Biedenharn was to recall later, "This provoked me no end. I gave my customers instead a box of lemons each, a sack of sugar and some coloring so they could make red lemonade for their farm hands.

"Since the soda water plant manager wouldn't accept the trade I offered him, I decided that I, too, could make a little money in soda water; so I wrote the Liquid Carbonic Company in St. Louis and bought an entire bottling outfit from them, second-hand—cases, bottling machinery, and all. In less than a month I was putting up my own soda water in bottles. I bottled lemon, strawberry, and sarsaparilla. I did all right with my soda water."

Biedenharn did all right with soda water, and he did all right with Coca-Cola, and it only took him until 1894 to figure out how to do more than all right by combining the two. "It was just that I saw the demand for Coca-Cola in town," he was later to say, "and I thought it would be profitable in the country *if I could only get it there.* I believed in bringing the product to the customer. I wanted to bring Coca-Cola to the country people outside the limits of the fountain. Even in the cities the fountains were limited in number and scattered here and there. I could see that many town folks wanted Coca-Cola, but it was not easily available."

Biedenharn's motives were obvious: "I found that the more Coca-Cola I was able to sell, the more I made out of it. This is why I began to push Coca-Cola and I pushed it as much as Asa Candler did." In fact, he pushed it more than Asa Candler, since Biedenharn sat down one day in the summer of 1894 and pushed it into a bottle.

"I just went to work and bottled Coca-Cola there in the Washington Street store where all the soda water equipment was located. I used the same equipment there for my soda water — a Liquid Carbonator and drum gas which I bought from Saratoga Springs. The first bottles for Coca-Cola were the old six-ounce Hutchinson stoppered bottles with the wire hook protruding from the neck when the stopper was pulled up. The necks of these bottles were short and were packed upside-down in the case.

"The city cases carried two dozen bottles, were full depth, with holes bored into a false bottom. These holes were just large enough for the neck of the bottle to pass through. The wooden cases, made of one-inch dressed lumber, had no partitions. Prices at that time were seventy cents per case for bottled Coca-Cola and sixty cents per case for bottled soda water.

"I know it is a fact that I was the first bottler of Coca-Cola in the world, because when I began there wasn't anybody bottling at that time. The soda water bottlers didn't want to bother with it; besides, they said the price for Coca-Cola was too high. They were merely content to make soda water.

"I never did say anything to Mr. Candler about it, but I did ship him the first two-dozen case of Coca-Cola I bottled. Mr. Candler immediately wrote back that it was fine. He made no further comment at all that I remember. You know, he never did return my bottles."

There is a terrific legend about Coca-Cola in which some character approaches Candler and demands a sum of money — $50,000 is the amount usually mentioned — for a "secret" which will make Candler rich. The money is forked over (this is the part that makes it a terrific story) and the man gives Candler the stunning secret: "Bottle it." But Biedenharn didn't get $50,000; he didn't even get his bottles back. Candler seemed to be ignoring the possibilities of the bottling business, even though others were not. One further example: on June 12, 1897 the Valdosta, Georgia *Daily Times* carried an advertisement which read:

HOLMES & BARBER, PROPS.
Manufacturers of
High-Grade Soda Water,
Ginger Ale, Ciders, etc.
We also put up Coca-Cola
in Bottles.
Prompt attention to all orders.
Families supplied with all goods
in special shapes for family trade.

Candler would not, however, be able to continue to ignore bottled Coca-Cola. During the Spanish-American War, a Chattanooga lawyer, serving in the commissary department of the Army in Cuba, noticed that Cubans bought great quantities of a bottled, carbonated, pineapple-flavored soft drink, Piña Fria. Why, thought Benjamin Franklin Thomas, couldn't Coca-Cola be bottled in such a manner?

Thomas, evidently unaware of the bottling already being done by Biedenharn and in Valdosta, returned to the United States after the end of the war and talked over his idea with a friend and fellow lawyer in Chattanooga, named Joseph Whitehead. Whitehead had a certain promotional bent, and he immediately saw the possibilities inherent in his friend's idea. The two men decided to go to Atlanta and gain the permission of The Coca-Cola Company to pursue their idea.

As they were readying themselves for the trip, it occurred to the men that they didn't know Asa Candler or for that matter, *any* executive of The Coca-Cola Company. Looking around for someone to give them an introduction, they hit on a friend of theirs, Sam Erwin, a clerk of the Chancery Court in Chattanooga, who turned out to be a first cousin of Asa Candler. They induced Erwin to accompany them to Atlanta and get them in to see Candler. (There is no record of what that inducement was, but whatever it was, it didn't make Erwin rich. He never owned stock in the bottling end of Coca-Cola, nor did he ever obtain a bottling franchise. He was to recall some 45 years later that, in 1899, he simply saw no future in bottled Coca-Cola.)

When Thomas and Whitehead met Candler, they found a man passionately involved with the fortunes of Coca-Cola syrup and almost completely disinterested in the bottling of his drink. In fact, Candler was more than disinterested; when he learned what Thomas and Whitehead wanted to do, he attempted to discourage them. One of the more unpleasant things about bottling of carbonated drinks during that period was the tendency of Hutchinson bottles to explode. But the two Chattanoogans were insistent, and assured Candler — this was obviously the area of his greatest worry — that they would accept full responsibility for the bottle domain.

Finally, on July 21, 1899, Candler and the two men signed a 600-word contract, which, while 598 words longer than the apocryphal "Bottle it," was in fact a far more astounding business agreement. The contract provided that Thomas and Whitehead were granted the right, in perpetuity, to bottle Coca-Cola. The two men paid no flat sum or royalty for this right: there was only the matter of $1.00 to be forked over to seal the bargain. (It never was.) They guaranteed to Candler (and it is easy to deduce from this just what it was about the bottling business that worried Candler) that they would establish bottling plants without any expense to The Coca-Cola Company and would assume all liabilities incurred by bottling plants. They further agreed to use only genuine Coca-Cola syrup, purchased from the Atlanta company at a fixed price, and to keep a supply adequate to meet demand. The Coca-Cola Company granted sole and exclusive rights to use of the trademark "Coca-Cola" so long as its use by the bottlers did not interfere with the soda fountain business of The Coca-Cola Company.

Thomas and Whitehead were given territorial rights to the entire United States, excepting Mississippi (Biedenharn's home grounds), Texas (another bottling agreement was being negotiated for Texas, though the negotiations would collapse after the Candler-Thomas-Whitehead contract was drawn up), and New England north of the New York-Connecticut line (a Boston firm, which was doing no bottling, had exclusive distribution rights to Coca-Cola in that area until 1912, and The Coca-Cola Company decided not to issue bottling franchises until expiration of this distribution contract).

The Chattanooga men went home with, as you can imagine, what they saw to be a blank cashier's check drawn on the account of America's thirst. Their next step was to start cashing that check, but to do that they had to set up bottling plants, and bottling plants cost money—about $5,000 each. Thomas had that amount of money; Whitehead didn't. But Whitehead had half of the contract for Coca-Cola and a friend named John Thomas Lupton, who was not only prescient but also wealthy. Lupton agreed to buy half of Whitehead's half for somewhere between $2,500 and $5,000. Thomas immediately set to work establishing a bottling plant in Chattanooga, which opened in late autumn of 1899.

The three partners realized that they themselves could not set up a network of plants to cover their territory. They agreed, therefore, to search for individuals who would be willing to invest their own capital in return for the exclusive right to bottle Coca-Cola in an area. This concept was to make a lot of men rich, as well as having the salutary effect of decentralizing the economic clout of Coca-Cola.

Soon after reaching this decision, however, Thomas and Whitehead had a series of differences which led them to agree to split their territory. One disagreement was in the color of the bottle. Thomas favored an amber container; Whitehead opted for a clear bottle. (The old Hutchinson bottle was by then being replaced by the crown and cork bottle, the kind that is still in use today, although the cork in the cap has since been replaced, in most cases, by plastic.) Much more important was the matter of the contracts. Thomas believed that potential bottlers should be limited to two-year contracts, thus providing a continuing review of each bottler's performance. Whitehead felt that better men could be induced to become Coca-Cola bottlers if the contracts were permanent. In any event, the splitting of the territory was accomplished by Whitehead drawing a division on a map and Thomas choosing one of the two resulting areas. Thomas chose an area which ran from Tennessee Northeast to the New York-Connecticut state line, but which also included California, Oregon, and Washington. Whitehead and Lupton got everything else (excepting Mississippi and New England, but including Texas). Thomas, of course, stayed in Chattanooga, and Whitehead moved to Atlanta, where he opened a bottling plant in 1900. (Lupton decided to live in Chattanooga.)

Within a year both Thomas and Whitehead began to disassociate themselves from the actual bottling operations they had started. They were finding it more profitable to operate as what were known as "Parent Bottlers," that is, the breast from which flowed the syrup to local bottlers. They made their money (and all three died multi-millionaires) by tacking a small mark-up onto the syrup they were buying from The Coca-Cola Company.

Naturally, Thomas and Whitehead wasted no time in awarding bottling contracts. Five plants were established in 1901, including ones in Chicago, Cincinnati, and Louisville. In 1902, 34 plants were started, 32 in 1903, 47 in 1904, 80 in 1905. By 1909 there were 379 local bottlers of Coca-Cola.

Soda fountain sales soared; and the bottling operation provided just that much more profit. In 1905, for example, the Atlanta company sold 1,548,888 gallons of syrup (at 128 drinks per gallon). Of that total, the bottlers took 452,511 gallons of Coca-Cola syrup. It was a bonanza for the reluctant Candler.

CHAPTER 3

The following trays, posters, and other advertising materials are not simply curious bits of nostalgia. The collective present day value of the stuff shown here is over $2500:

Lillian Nordica, a turn-of-the century opera star, was portrayed on serving trays and coupon cards redeemable for a free Coke. This 1904 tray is worth over $100 today.

The certificate for 500 shares of the Company was signed over to the new owners in 1919 for $25,000,000. By 1929 the firm was netting that much each year. Evidently the Candler family had forgotten the promised therapeutic benefits of Coke, as shown in the first calendar advertising the drink.

The National Temperance Drink

25c. **HIRES IMPROVED ROOT BEER** 25c.
IN LIQUID. NO BOILING OR STRAINING EASILY MADE.
THIS PACKAGE MAKES FIVE GALLONS

Hires
REGISTERED
IMPROVED
Rootbeer
Charles E. Hires Co., Philadelphia, U.S.A.

Drink it ——
and the world drinks with you.

Hires Rootbeer—drink it and enjoy its delicious flavor—its sparkling snap and effervescence—drink it, and derive the benefit of its health-giving properties. Soothing to the nerves, vitalizing to the blood, refreshing to the brain, beneficial in every way. Hires Rootbeer gives the children strength to resist the enervating effects of the heat, bridges the convalescent over the trying part of a hot day, helps even a cynic to see the brighter side of life. One package of Hires makes five gallons, and there is more fun than trouble in making it.

Hires Rootbeer, carbonated, is put up in sterilized bottles ready for drinking. When you are touring awheel, journeying on the train, dining at the hotel or café, a bottle of this delicious beverage will make you feel at home.

HIRES Rootbeer

Carbonated, in cases of two dozen pint bottles. Sold everywhere.
See that Hires and the signature, Charles E. Hires, are on each bottle.

THE CHARLES E. HIRES CO., Philadelphia

Hires Root Beer, which first was promoted at the Philadelphia Exposition of 1876, for many years used the unlikely visage of this small child in its ads and on its trays. Why they did not find a more appealing subject is open to speculation. This ad was on the back cover of the June, 1897, Ladies Home Journal.

Hamilton King painted "The Coca-Cola Girl" of 1909 (left) while N. C. Wyeth painted the gorgeous scene at right for the 1937 calendar.

DRINK
DELICIOUS
Coca-Cola

THE COCA-COLA GIRL

Around 1905, a local bottler of Coke, the Western Coca-Cola Bottling Co., located, as one might expect, in Chicago, began to put out its own advertising items. This flip-down trade card infuriated Asa Candler, not so much for the quasi-nudity, but because it said Coke was a great mixer for liquor.

A glass of *Coca-Cola* is just as enjoyable as the play itself
Delightfully in harmony with the spirit of all recreations, it is a delicious, refreshing tonic-beverage in which a proposal to health and happiness becomes an accomplished fact.

Massingale of Atlanta, which was the first ad agency for Coke, produced this ad, which ran in the September, 1906, American Theater.

The racy poster (very racy, when you think about it) was done c. 1907 by the Chicago bottler. In the early '20s, Hires was still claiming purity for the drink.

"SATISFIED"

This turn-of-the-century poster was almost certainly not commissioned by Dr. Pepper (or the nymphs most likely would have been holding bottles of the drink). It was probably a commercial litho onto which the company added its logo.

One of the most famous slogans for Coke, dreamed up by crack ad man Archie Lee, made its first appearance in the February, 1922 issue of Ladies Home Journal. This ad marked the first time Coke was advertised as being a year-round drink.

INVITING
You

Coca-Cola has a wonderful winning way. In it you find the happy answer to thirst. A taste thrill. A quick, wholesome little lift when you need one.

This drink just naturally fits into a pause from work or play.... Tastes good when nothing else does.... Leaves you cool and refreshed.

Only 5¢. Always the same high quality.

THE COCA-COLA COMPANY
ATLANTA, GA.

Drink
Coca-Cola

THE DRINK THAT MAKES A   PAUSE REFRESHING

JEAN HARLOW
Howard Hughes Star

In retrospect, Jean Harlow may seem a bit, ah, overly sexy, to have been used to advertise Coke. Can it be that at the time she was just another pretty face? This ad appeared in a 1935 issue of Photoplay.

Ads for Coke
have been
known for their
inspired
graphics,
as evidenced
by this 1926
wall hanger and
a1946 award-
winning poster.

A Hires
cardboard
bottle hanger
dating from
the
mid-twenties.

Haddon
Sundbloom
created
the great
mythic Santa
for Coke in
1931. Later
on (facing page)
Pepsi hired its
own mythic
personality,
Norman
Rockwell,
to do a
Santa in the
1950s.

CHAPTER 4

By 1904, Candler and The Coca-Cola Company could well afford to hire an advertising agency. Though Pemberton's original $73.96 advertising expenditure in 1886 did not pay—it attracted $160 in retail sales, but Pemberton grossed only $25 for the bulk syrup—nevertheless, his successors were unstinting in their efforts to promote their product.

The Coca-Cola Company's cumulative advertising expenditure through 1903 was $762,502.65; by that year it was spending around $200,000 annually, and increasing that amount in direct ratio to sales. Artwork was being produced primarily for point-of-sale items—metal serving trays for fount men and change trays, or paper trade cards and free sample cards. Newspaper advertising, which had started with the standard practice of one-column cuts (that could do little more than feature the trademark "Coca-Cola" in script) was still at the mercy of the smear of black-and-white newsprint. But around 1900, national magazines were able for the first time to print four-color on the inside of the magazine. This made them attractive to Candler and Dobbs, the more so since magazines were classier than the penny, yellow journalism which passed for newspapers in much of America.

The first magazine ad for Coca-Cola appeared in *Munsey's* in 1902, but it was obvious that the Company needed professional help in creating advertisements which would function far from the place where a sale might actually take place. Choosing an appropriate agency was an old-shoe bit of business: Candler just walked down the road a ways and engaged the Massengale agency in Atlanta. Today there are precious few Massengale ads kicking around—back copies of 1905 magazines not being a glut on any market—but those few that can be found (an excellent source is the *American Theater* Magazine, circa 1906) show that Massengale was trying to create an image for Coca-Cola. The art, often produced by Henry Hutt, would indeed show the obvious—people drinking Coca-Cola—but he attempted to carve out a sociological niche for his characters. They were middle- to upper-middle class, enjoying themselves on outings (or, in the case of the *American Theater* ads, at soda fountains in theaters). Somehow there was always a refreshment stand in the background of the scene, no matter how sylvan the area where the main characters appeared. Massengale also attempted to come up with slogans to replace the already well-worn "Delicious and Refreshing." Under the Coke logo, there was always the message, "Sold at all founts and carbonated in bottles, 5¢." The trademark Coca-Cola would be tagged with what was supposed to be a snappy phrase, as in "Coca-Cola adds a refreshing relish to every form of exercise." Or: "Coca-Cola is a delicious beverage delightfully in harmony with the spirit of all outings." Massengale didn't last long. Great numbers of streetcar card advertising salesmen called on the Coca-Cola Company, which was spending lots of money in streetcars (a whopping $107,000 in 1909). One of these men was an aggressive fellow from St. Louis named W. C. D'Arcy. D'Arcy made his pitch for the transit lines he represented, and got business; but more importantly, he managed to sell himself to Dobbs and Candler. (One can surmise from the fact that D'Arcy called on Dobbs and Candler rather than Massengale, that the ad agency was not itself aggressive enough to consolidate its position as the sole representative for the advertising of Coca-Cola.)

Dobbs, in particular, liked D'Arcy's style so much that he urged D'Arcy to form an advertising agency, one which Dobbs was prepared to back with an order for $2,500 in Coca-Cola advertising to be placed in Texas; moreover, Dobbs promised all the additional business D'Arcy could handle.

D'Arcy was no dummy, and on August 23, 1906, he got into the advertising business, handling part of the Coca-Cola account. Massengale was not ditched immediately, and so for a few years The Coca-Cola Company had two agencies. Since each agency was paid commission only on those ads it produced and placed, it became necessary to be able to differentiate between the two. Massengale signed its ads, while D'Arcy stuck a little "D" with an arrow through it in his ads. (D'Arcy got a little hung up on the symbol of the arrow, so that even after he no longer had to sign ads, he used the arrow, making it bigger and bigger, and working it into a slogan, "Whenever you see an arrow, think of Coca-Cola." It was lucky for Coca-Cola that D'Arcy hadn't signed his ads with a picture of an elephant.)

Both D'Arcy and Massengale got into the business of soliciting testimonials, being careful, of course, to stay the hell away from doctors or any medical men. Massengale, with an experience gained from those ads in *American Theater,* produced, naturally enough, a theatrical ad: "An Act Not on the Bill—Coca-Cola—The 'Star' Performance. Much depends upon how you come prepared to play your part on the stage of life, as well as on the theatrical stage. Coca-Cola prevents fatigue incident to earnest and arduous work, whether in the bright glare of the lime-light or in the humbler walks of life, and makes it possible for you to make your appearance with light step, sparkling eye, steady hand and nerves, and, above all, with a clear head capable of lucid thinking and logical reasoning.

"Eddie Foy, famous laugh provoker in *The Orchid,* says: 'After a long, trying rehearsal, I find nothing that will relieve fatigue like Coca-Cola. Both in my Work and in my Play, it is the most refreshing and delicious drink I know.'

"Delicious! Thirst-Quenching! Refreshing! 5¢—Sold Everywhere. Guaranteed under the Pure Food and Drug Act, June 20, 1906, serial number 3324."

Well, that was okay, but the business about "relieving fatigue," while it could very well have been nothing more than an innocent reference to the sugar in Coca-Cola, still reminded one of the old, medicinal days. Reading the copy of one of D'Arcy's testimonial ads will clearly show why Massengale got the ax. Under a picture of a baseball player at bat, was the headline:

"Ty Cobb at the Bat. Something's bound to happen. Everybody on edge—nerve a-tingle—head whizzing. Crack!! Good boy Ty!! Safe!! And then you shout yourself hoarse. When it's all over you're hot, thirsty and limp. A cold, snappy drink of Coca-Cola will put you back into the game—relieve the thirst and cool you off. Rooters and ball players swear by it.

"Ty Cobb Says: 'I drink Coca-Cola regularly throughout all seasons of the year. On days when we are playing a double-header I always find that a drink of Coca-Cola between the games refreshes me to such an extent that I can start the second game, feeling as if I had not been exercising at all, in spite of my exertions in the first.'

"Delicious—Refreshing—Thirst-Quenching. Get the genuine. 5¢ Everywhere."

Obviously, D'Arcy was not limiting his agency to magazines. In 1908, he and Sam Dobbs (as well, perhaps, as Frank Robinson), dreamed up the idea for what was to become at that time the world's largest animated outdoor sign. It was erected on the main line of the Pennsylvania Railroad between Philadelphia and New York. Standing 32 feet high, it showed a young man drawing Coca-Cola syrup into a glass from the kind of porcelain dispensing urn which the Company in those days gave to retailers; the snapper, of course, was that real water (representative of carbonated water, and obtained by running a two-inch pipe some four hundred feet to a water main) flowed out of the fountain. Nor were the dreams of D'Arcy earthbound. In 1909 he hired a dirigible to fly over the city of Washington with a huge "Coca-Cola" painted on the sides.

With everything going so well—by 1909 Coca-Cola was cited by the Associated Advertising Clubs of America as "the best advertised article in America," which was certainly due in part to the fact that the Company was spending $761,981.35 on advertising in that year alone (or, as much in that one year as it had spent in all the years between 1886 and 1903)—it was time for disaster to strike.

In 1909 representatives of the Federal Government seized a quantity of Coca-Cola syrup which was in transit to the Thomas Parent Bottler in Chattanooga. The Feds went into court

52.

(The United States v. 40 Barrels and 20 Kegs of Coca-Cola) in Chattanooga, claiming that Coca-Cola violated provisions of the Pure Food and Drug Act, a claim which rested on the preposterously narrow notion that, since Coca-Cola was not made up *exclusively* of extract of kola nut and coca leaf, to call it Coca-Cola was mislabelling. If that seems a nonsensical reason to haul a company into court, it is well to remember that, while we are in theory a nation of laws, those laws are administered by people, and are therefore subject to the normal run of witlessness, decency, ego, humaneness, gall and unvarnished prejudice.

The trial was held in open court and received extensive press coverage, providing, in fact, banner headlines day-after-day in the Chattanooga papers. At times it almost seemed, from the standpoint of jurisprudence, to be nothing short of a freak show on the part of the government; the prosecution seemed more interested in learning the makeup of the secret ingredients in Coca-Cola than in winning its case.

Coca-Cola was acquitted, a precedent-setting blessing for such upcoming products as Mustang automobiles and *Time* Magazine. There were, however, some unsettling side effects to the trial. A great number of people around the country had been sitting around bitten with envy as Asa Candler got rich off a simple 5¢ drink. Obviously, anyone could cook up a cola-flavored drink, and a lot of people did, many of them calmly naming their products after Coca-Cola — sort of. There was "Coca Nola" and "Koke Ola" (even "Fletcher's Coca-Cola") and God knows how many other drinks, all of which left Harold Hirsch, general counsel of The Coca-Cola Company, very busy, and all of which left the public unimpressed.

One would-be challenger popped up after the Chattanooga trial with credentials that purported to go far beyond an attempt to capitalize on the name Coca-Cola through simple alliteration. A Savannah woman named Diva Brown issued a pamphlet in which she claimed that it was she, along with two other associates, who had bought the assets of the Pemberton Chemical Company, including, naturally, the formula for Coca-Cola. After the sale was effected, she said, Pemberton informed her and her partners that he had neglected to tell them that he had *previously* sold the formula for Coca-Cola. This, said Mrs. Brown, left her group with, among other things, the formula for Coca-Cola but no right to market it under that name. So, she said, she had gone ahead and produced a drink, first called Yum-Yum and then called Vera-Coca, which was exactly the same as Coca-Cola except for one thing—it was cheaper. Mrs. Brown pointed out that purchasers of Coca-Cola syrup were clearly paying for such items as a building which The Coca-Cola Company was erecting in New York City. (In fact, Candler was putting it up on his own.)

While the pamphlet probably had no good effect on Asa Candler's digestion, it ended on a terribly poignant, plaintive note. After a final rumble of drums: "Now, if you have let the facts herein set forth sink in—if an overwhelming truth has swept before it all of doubt and hesitation, permit us to fill the glass in your one hand with Coca-Cola and in the other with Vera-Coca, while you weigh them in the balance"; there came a full whiff of the blues: "Vera-Coca is now being sold under the name of Quencher. Order Quencher today." Quencher was as big a hit as Vera-Coca and Yum-Yum.

During this time D'Arcy was busily inserting in its advertisements a line asking the public to "Demand the genuine" or "Accept no substitutes" or to "Demand the genuine by full name—nicknames encourage substitution". (The agency had also, in conjunction with the Company, felt compelled to offer, at the time of the Chattanooga acquittal, a booklet explaining the Coca-Cola triumph.) Of course, the best way to "defend" Coca-Cola was to go about selling an enormous amount of it, so D'Arcy began to blitz America with advertising.

In 1913, for example, a year in which the advertising budget for Coca-Cola was over $1,399,000, the Company distributed the following:

200,000	4-head cutouts for window display
5,000,000	Lithographed metal signs from 6″ x 10″ to 5′ x 8′
10,000	Enamel metal signs 12″ x 36″, 18″ x 45″
60,000	Fountain festoons
250,000	Special signs for bottlers 12″ x 36″
50,000	Cardboard cutouts for window display
35,000	Seashore cutouts for window display

60,000	4-head festoons for soda fountains
10,000	Lithograph metal signs
20,000	Lithograph metal displays containing reproduction of bottles
50,000	Metal signs for tacking under windows
200,000	Fiber signs for tacking on walls of refreshment stands
2,000,000	Trays for soda fountains
50,000	Window trims
250,000	5-head window displays and mirror decorations
1,000,000	Japanese fans
50,000	Christmas wreath and bell decorations for fountains
50,000	The Coca-Cola Company song (sheet music)
1,000,000	Calendars
50,000	Thermometers
10,000,000	Match books
50,000,000	Doilies (paper)
10,000	Large calendars for business offices
144,000	Pencils
20,000,000	Blotters
10,000	Framed metal signs for wall displays
5,000	Transparent globes mosaic art glass work
■ 25,000,000	Baseball score cards ■

Unfortunately, exact figures have been lost on the amount distributed of the following items, also put out that year: 24-sheet posters for 10′ x 20′ billboards; oil cloth signs for store fronts; transparent signs for windows and transoms; art glass signs (these, the globes mentioned above, and lamps in the same style are what are known today as "Tiffany" items); and celluloid display cards.

Strangely enough, even with all of this activity, it was not W. C. D'Arcy or Asa Candler or Sam Dobbs who was to come up with what would be, after the trademark itself, the most far-reaching and famous identification for Coca-Cola. It was some men in Indiana, acting on a request that had originated with Ben Thomas in Chattanooga.

CHAPTER 5

Obviously, one of the most important elements in the success of Coca-Cola was the matter of product identification. It was crucial to the Company that someone drinking Coca-Cola be involved in a small paradox: while Coca-Cola was supposed to be a beverage which, taken casually, lent an element of relaxation and refreshment (if there were a better word, don't you think the Company would have used it?) to normal activities, still, the drinking of it could not be all *that* casual. The guy sitting there with a glass of Coke was supposed to be completely aware that he was drinking a Coke, an awareness which could not be left completely to the vagaries of fineness in the individual palate.

One of the ways to do this in a soda fountain was to serve Coca-Cola on metal serving trays with the name of the drink and a picture on each tray, give change on similar, though smaller, trays, and fill the walls with various signs advertising Coke. Another way, adopted after 1899, was to put the drink in a glass which itself advertised the drink. The Company had been distributing straight-sided soda fountain glasses as early as 1890, and calling them Coca-Cola glasses, but the only thing which marked them as such were hash lines that measured the level for the syrup. Around 1899 the words Coca-Cola were added to the glass, and the shape was changed, the glass flaring out at the top. Sometime around 1910 the

D'Arcy arrow motif was added to the glass, in the form of a "5¢" that was shaped from an arrow (page 66).

While all of that worked well for the soda fountain trade, it didn't do much for the bottlers. Though all the bottles used had the trademark Coca-Cola script blown into the glass, the bottles differed. There was the matter of the Thomas amber vs. the White-head clear. Some bottlers even took that damned D'Arcy arrow and blew *it* onto the side of the bottle. Furthermore, the diamond-shaped paper labels tended to fall off when a cold bottle sweated on a hot day.

Ben Thomas had started buttonholing people in his organization as early as 1905, saying, over and over again, that Coca-Cola should be contained in a bottle which was uniform and so recognizable that a customer would know he was holding one in the dark, or know he was seeing a Coke bottle even if the bottle was broken. Thomas' wish had to wait on refinements in the bottle-blow-ing process, so it wasn't until 1913 that all Coca-Cola bottle suppliers were asked to submit new designs to the Company. There were two requirements for the bottle. It had to be capable of being produced by machinery then in use, and it had to be distinctive.

In Terre Haute, Indiana, Chapman J. Root, whose Root Glass Company was a major supplier of Coca-Cola bottles, called together key members of his staff and told them of the request. His superintendent, a Swede named Alex Samuelson (who was also a noted machine designer), headed a group assigned to come up with an entry. Samuelson, who had previously invented various glass-blowing techniques which had advanced the state of the indus-try's art, promptly turned the spadework over to a cost accountant named T. Clyde Edwards. Samuelson wanted as much information as possible on the cola nut and the coca leaf, thinking that perhaps a design could be created that would have something to do with the two most famous ingredients of Coke.

T. Clyde, unsung hero, *shlepped* over to the library, where—legend has it—he found a line drawing of a cola nut in an encyclopedia. It showed a bulging pod with longitudinal ridges and it looked, when you come right down to it, more like a cocoa pod than a cola nut. A mold shop operator named Earl R. Dean copied this drawing and took it to Samuelson. Samuelson, who realized that the shape could be adapted to a workable design—one that could be easily molded and would work well as a bottle—promptly executed a basic design (page 65). After modifications, the final design was patented in Samuelson's name in November, 1915, and submitted, along with some 30 other entries, to a panel of seven parent bottlers the next year. After almost a week of deliberation, the bottlers chose the Samuelson design, which went into production late in 1916.

No one knows what T. Clyde or Earl Dean or Samuelson got, but Chapman Root, *he* got. The contract which turned the design over to The Coca-Cola Company in order that it could be licensed to other bottle makers (Root Glass making good money just from *its* production of Coca-Cola bottles) specified a royalty of 5¢ per gross paid to Root. If that appears a breathtaking figure, consider the fact that Root *declined* an offer of 25¢ a gross.

Things could not have been going too much better for Asa Candler. By 1916 his Company was selling 9,715,892 gallons of syrup, which brought in a cool $13,182,940.99; the Company was spending $1,717,941.86 in advertising that year. The retail figures were staggering: 1,243,634,176 drinks (or 3,407,216 a day) which generated a retail volume of $62,181,709. Candler was 63. He had devoted himself to Coca-Cola for 26 years, and even though he had had to weather a lot of misery, it had made him rich. He was at an age and station in life when he could be persuaded to look beyond his corporate activities. The persuading came in the form of a group of Atlantans who asked him to run for mayor. Candler thought about it and then resigned the Company presidency to his son Howard. He was easily elected to a two-year term as mayor in 1916.

It seemed that Asa Candler was no sooner out the door of The Coca-Cola Company than things began to go bad for the firm. The war, of course, affected the Company's sales. For the first time in its history, less Coca-Cola was sold in a year than in the year preceding. D'Arcy, of course, publicly explained why:

"Victory's Reward means Volume Restored. To every American business which, at the expense of quantity, maintained the full quality of its product throughout the war, peace brings restoration of normal volume.

"When conservation cut our allotment of sugar in two, we cut down our output of Coca-Cola one-half in order to maintain its quality at 100 percent. Nothing changed, cheapened, nor diluted, Coca-Cola remained 'all there' from the beginning of the war to the end.

"Pending readjustment of the world's sugar supply, our output of Coca-Cola will remain limited until the need of conservation shall no longer exist. Meanwhile Coca-Cola will live up to its past, and we, in common with other American business, look hopefully to restoration of the happy normal."

The pending normal that they were looking for was not at all that happy. The "need of conservation" would disappear with the end of the war, true, but so would the emergency measures that had frozen the price of sugar at 5½¢ a pound. It was obvious to everyone that the price of sugar would soar after the war (Cuba offered to freeze the price at 6½¢ but was turned down). Such a price rise would be a dire crisis for the Company, for however much palaver had been expended about the coca and the cola in Coca-Cola, however much people had wondered about the secret ingredients in the drink, the fact was that Coca-Cola depended most on two basic ingredients, sugar and water. By 1919 the Company was caught between a sugar price that was jumping from 6¢ to 10¢ to 12¢ a pound, and the sacrosanct 5¢ retail price of the drink.

With Asa out of the Company, the rest of the Candler family began to feel that their gold mine was in clear danger of petering out — and petering out rather abruptly at that. They began to talk of selling the business.

The sugar crisis was not the only trouble besetting the Candler family and Coca-Cola. The Candlers believed that the Company was in grave danger of losing a major court case, a matter of trademark infringement, one in a long series the Company had been forced to file over the years. The defendant in this case was The Koke Company of America. In the years 1910–1916, the Company had spent $11,288,278.26 for advertising, a good portion of which went to beating into the public consciousness that Coca-Cola should be ordered by full name only. The nickname which the public was being implored to avoid was "Coke." Obviously, part of the Company's apparent priggishness regarding the nickname stemmed from the fact that lower-case "coke" was short for cocaine, and who in Company headquarters in Atlanta wanted to be reminded of *that?* Also, it was probable that Company officials really believed that use of "Coke" would dilute the strength of "Coca-Cola," and would therefore aid competitors.

But there was another reason why The Coca-Cola Company resisted "Coke," one which has never been admitted by the Company, probably because no one in the Company has ever been fully conscious of it. The purpose of any nickname is to simplify the saying of a given word or words, or to graft onto a name a more suggestive or catchy title.

"Coke" was and is, after all, a simplification, but it is probable that no one in The Coca-Cola Company ever felt that "Coca-Cola" needed simplification. This was *not* merely a matter of over-possessive pride in "Coca-Cola," but a matter of pronunciation. The Northerner who approaches saying "Coca-Cola," is approaching four syllables, the first two of which take some time to speak because the mouth, puckered forward for the "co-", has to be drawn back for the "-ca", and then pushed forward again for the second "co-". The Southerner either drops the "-ca" entirely or brings it out as a tiny gargle, hinted at rather than dwelt on, especially when hurried, so that what you hear sounds like "ko-kola."

Fittingly enough, the best way to have observed this phenomenon of dialect was by dialing the main switchboard number of The Coca-Cola Company in Atlanta prior to 1971. The operators, fielding a blizzard of calls, almost *always* answered your ring with "ko-kola." Recently, however, Southern Bell has installed new equipment for the corporation which allows an outside caller to dial directly into the extension he wishes to speak to. With the number of incoming calls to the main board lessened, the operators have enough time to gargle out that final "-ca" in "coca-."

If the Candlers *were* proceeding from the assumption that "Coke" was not a matter of simplification (because "Coca-Cola" didn't need any), then the nickname had to be detrimental, in one way or another, to the Company and the drink. This, of course, did not stop people from asking for Coke — the advertising couldn't stop them either; it did, however, seem to play into the hands of The Koke Company of America, because The Coca-Cola Company was put in the incredibly awful position of trying to deny the other company the use of a name (or the phonetic version of a name), which The Coca-Cola Company had publicly opposed for use in describing its own drink. It is obvious why the Candlers thought they would lose — and why they wanted to sell. Only Asa didn't want to sell: His term as mayor expired, but he never returned to active participation in the Company. So, despite his many objections, his family finally won him over. (Strictly speaking, they didn't have to bother. They held the stock.) A group of banks — Chase National and Guaranty Trust of New York, as well as The Trust Company of Georgia — agreed to buy the Company for $25 million. The bankers were led by the head of the Georgia bank, Ernest Woodruff.

People who care for irony can probably choke on the ironies connected with the ownership of Coca-Cola. Pemberton dumped it, it passed through several hands until it got to Candler, and then after it had made him rich, Candler went and unloaded it. (Candler had unloaded a veritable tidal wave of Coke during his years of ownership: 104 million gallons, the equivalent of over 13 billion individual drinks, with a retail value of some $565.8 million pre-1920 dollars.)

If the Candler family folded when it should have stood pat, it was possibly because the family had forgotten, or never really believed, Asa's first major ad for Coke in the 1890 *Grier's Almanac,* the one in which he painted the virtues of the "wonderful nerve and brain tonic." A good nerve tonic was obviously what the Candlers needed in 1919.

Still, however shaky the Company seemed to them as they disposed of it, it was far and away the preeminent leader in soft drinks.

POP.

CHAPTER 6

When you get to the illustrations of the various delivery trucks for Coke and Dr. Pepper, think about the Dodge and Ford vans you may have seen recently, painted bright red and sporting the new swirl logo for Coke. What an investment one of those would be!

The original model for the hobble skirt Coca-Cola bottle was created in 1915. Because the model was too wide for manufacturing equipment of the period (and probably for some aesthetic reasons), the shape was slimmed down to what we know today. Only two of these prototypes are known to exist.

The four stage
transmutation
of the Coke
glass. The one
at left is
c.1915, with
the D'Arcy
-inspired arrow
etched into it.
The syrup line
disappeared as
soda jerks began
to use the
pre-mix machine.
The change
from flared
to bell-shape
reduced
breakage.
Bottom, three
variations of
the Pepsi
bottle. The
bottle at far
left looked
very much like
another famous
soda pop bottle,
a coincidence?

A dispenser for
Orange Crush,
c. 1930.

A lithographed metal Orange Crush door pusher from 1926. The RC bottle is circa 1945.

This ceramic Hires syrup jug is c. 1900-20. Today, it sells for upwards of $100.

This dispenser for Lash's is a "XXth Century" Cooler, patented in 1908. One of the nozzles was for the orange syrup; the other was to bleed off the ice water which surrounded the syrup container.

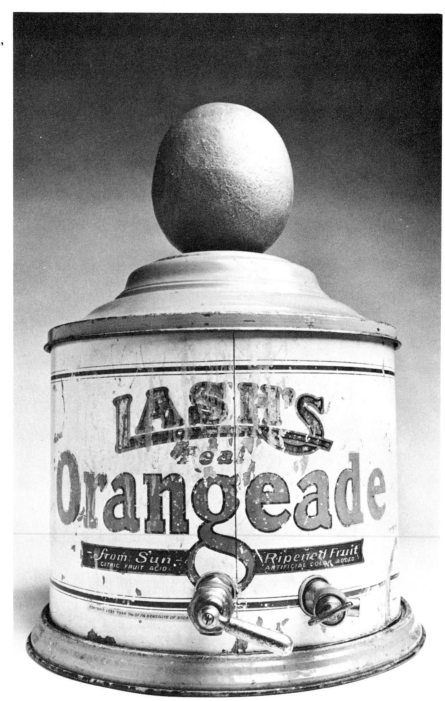

Drugstores were provided with a staggering number of cardboard cutouts. This one dates from 1941.

DRINK Coca-Cola

TAKE OFF... REFRESHED

The upper
cutout
was used
in the midst of
World War II,
natch. The one
at bottom (love
that squirrel)
dates from
1926.

Weird stuff. The ad people were always trying out scenes within scenes. Ironically, the illustration of the girl wound up being the 1917 calendar, with the model being known as "The World War I Girl." The 1916 calendar featured film star Pearl White.

Drugstores are always pop art heaven. The one at top, on the corner of Green Bay and Atkinson in Milwaukee, was shot in 1934. Note the NRA eagle. Pardee Drugs stood at the corner of Wilshire Blvd. and La Brea in Los Angeles.

The sailor was on a wall in Baltimore in 1935. The neon spectacular was capable of forecasting a full range of weather.

7-Up was first marketed as a hangover remedy. This ad dates from the early '30s.

The 1933
outdoor sign for
Moxie features
the famous old
Moxiemobile,
which actually
had a rider up
there on the
horse which was
grafted onto the
car. Snazzy!
The Coca-Cola
truck was
illustrated in a
1932 booklet
to show the
bottlers what
standard colors
were.

Dr. Pepper was first delivered by Wells Fargo wagons, as befitted a Texas soda pop. Later, of course, they got their own wheels. Any one of the vehicles used by Coke bottlers (at left) would be worth its weight in gold today.

Leaded,
stained glass
chandeliers
were
distributed to
soda founts
between 1905
and 1920.

CHAPTER 7

Coca-Cola, of course, was not the only soft drink of the period. Candler's success had inspired dozens of pharmacists to start cooking up their own syrups, while bottlers across the country tried to emulate the sales growth of bottled Coke by introducing various brands of cola and non-cola drinks. The obvious temptation was to try and take a ride on the promotional work already done for Coke by providing a competitor with a confusingly similar name. This tactic almost always backfired, with the competing drink losing, not in the marketplace, but in the courtroom.

Other flavors fared somewhat better. Ginger ale had been bottled as early as the 1880s, but had to wait on the introduction of Cliquet Club and Goldelle's in the early 1900s (and later Canada Dry) for brand names which would aid in carrying the generic drink into a center spot in the public consciousness. Root beer was most notably represented by Hires, a product of the Charles E. Hires Company of Philadelphia. Hires was catapulted into prominence at the Philadelphia Centennial Exposition of 1876, when packages of the dried roots, barks, and herbs which made up the extract of the drink were exhibited and mixed into the finished beverage.

Hires was soon being advertised and sold as an ex-

81.

tract, and within ten years was available ready to drink in bottles. Its advertising, however, continued to emphasize the rather dubious advantages of home brewing for the next twenty years. (The only real advantage was in price, the extract being far less expensive than a 5¢ bottle of a finished drink. Hires, however, evidently thought that people were terribly worried about sanitary conditions in bottling plants; and people were, bottling plants of the period being notoriously filthy. What Hires did not understand were the risks Americans would take in the name of convenience.)

Although Hires followed the lead of Coca-Cola in various merchandising and advertising ideas—Hires distributed trade cards, earthenware mugs with its name on them, and metal carrying trays—most of them were, from the point-of-view of advertising effectiveness, inferior to those of Coca-Cola. Many of the Hires trade cards, for example, used religious pictures as the art work. A typical card had a lithograph of a religious scene and a scriptural quotation on the front. On the back, it said:

"This is a famous picture, a familiar sight to European connoisseurs, but not so well known here. It is the best copy extant of that exquisite oil painting 'Ruth and Naomi.'

"All the pathos of this touching episode of Scripture is here—the local color, the sentiment. It is another reading by the light of inspiration.

"The artistic beauty of the pleading attitude, the tenderness of expression, and the womanly warmth cannot be too much admired. It is enough to say that they have never been surpassed.

"In his travels abroad, our Mr. Charles E. Hires secured a copy of this work, and at a cost of over $5,000 we have had it reproduced with scrupulous exactness by lithography.

"This masterpiece of lithographic art is offered as a Souvenir to the patrons of Hires Root Beer, and should be accorded a place in the drawing-room.

"Send us Five Labels like this, (25¢ Hires' Improved Root Beer! In Liquid, No Boiling or Straining. Easily Made. This Package Makes Five Gallons.), cut from the front of the package, and we will send you free, for framing, one of these 'Ruth and Naomi' pictures, size 15 x 20 inches, without advertisement."

After the address, almost as an afterthought, the following lines were appended: "What's the difference?

"You drink Hires' Root Beer for pleasure and get a tonic.

"You take it as a tonic and get pleasure. It is wholesome, sparkling, and effervescent. Just the thing for making health and pure blood."

While Hires was wrapping itself in the Bible (using God to sell pop was, in retrospect, pretty tacky), some of its non-religious promotional work managed to be equally unappealing. One of its most heralded identification marks was the picture of a small child — at least, what one must assume was a small, child, since the creature most nearly resembled a side show dwarf—holding a mug of Hires. Hardly the best recommendation for a product, and on a par with Hires' oft-repeated boast of being made up of "roots, barks, and herbs." Those ingredients mentioned in advertising for Coca-Cola always had an exotic air about them; roots, barks, and herbs were not only not exotic, but, if you thought about them, a trifle distasteful.

The second-oldest major brand of soda pop was concocted by a young man who was working at a pharmacy in Virginia around 1880. The young man, a soda jerk, had eyes for the pharmacist's daughter, a match-up celebrated in fiction but frowned on in fact. The pharmacist threw the young man out.

Jobless and a go-getter, the kid did what any red-blooded American would do in such circumstances — he went West, winding up in a town that served as a way station between Dallas and Austin: Waco. The kid got a job, naturally enough, at The Old Corner Drug Store in Waco, where he experimented with a number of new soft drink formulations. Legend has it that he left Waco to go back and marry the pharmacist's daughter in Virginia, but that is just legend, since we don't even know the young man's name. Whether or not he ever got the girl, he immortalized her father, because Texans, tired of hearing him moon over his Virginia romance, dubbed his best soft drink Dr. Pepper, the name of the Virginia pharmacist.

After the kid left town, a Waco chemist named R. S. Lazenby started experimenting with the basic formula that he had been drinking at The Old Corner Drug Store. Two years later, in 1885, he put the drink on sale commercially. It was advertised as "The King of Beverages, Free From Caffeine," and though its proprietors today say that it is not a cola, it did taste something like a very peppy cherry Coke.

Dr. Pepper was regional, and didn't make much of a splash until the mid-'20s, when the company came across a Columbia University professor named Walter Eddy. Eddy was doing nutritional research, and had found that people's energy dropped off mid-way between meals. He recommended, in a book called *The Liquid Bite* (which from its title alone sounds as if it were underwritten by soft drink manufacturers), that people take a shot of glucose at 10 a.m., 2 p.m., and 4 p.m. Naturally enough, the easiest way to get that glucose was not simply by sucking on some granulated sugar, but by buying a soft drink. Dr. Pepper immediately adopted a slogan, "Drink a Bite to Eat at 10, 2, and 4 o'clock." It wasn't too catchy, but it provided the basis for a clock symbol blown onto Dr. Pepper bottles with three hands, pointing at the magic hours.

It appeared, prior to the end of World War I, that Coca-Cola might be challenged in the marketplace by Moxie, a drink which had its home in Boston (New England, recall, was penetrated most slowly by Coca-Cola because of the restrictive distribution contract). Moxie advertised itself as a "nerve food" and is said to have tasted rather like a mixture of root beer, black cherry wishniak, and cola. Moxie's fortunes, however, disappeared as a result of the post-war sugar debacle, and a terrible error in judgment on the part of the drink's proprietors: they allowed the name to slip out of upper case and into common usage, an error that was compounded by the fact that lower-case moxie did not automatically suggest the drink. Moxie survived, but only as a regional drink.

The history of soda pop, like the history of American automobile manufacturing, is littered with dozens of brand names which never quite made it: Egyptian Mystery — The Drink of the Ages; Charleston Pop; Tip 2 Lip; Kold Kup; Bruce's Juices; Coo Coo; Red Head Flapper; Princesa; Ten Pins; Orange-e-Tang. Some brands flourished as regional drinks: Dr. Brown's in New York (Brown's

Cel-Ray was and is recommended as a drink which compliments Jewish delicatessen food); Cott's in Philadelphia.

It is possible, however, that the pre-eminence of Coca-Cola came from something at once simple but inexplicable: a national preference for the taste of a cola drink. Given this possibility, the greatest danger to Coca-Cola lay in a drink which had been developed by a man who was in many ways reminiscent of Pemberton and Candler, a New Bern, North Carolina, pharmacist named Caleb Bradham.

Bradham had been mixing fountain drinks for customers of his pharmacy since he went into business in 1893. At some point in the next years he developed a formula which was more appealing to his customers than any other; in 1898 he began to call it Pepsi-Cola. It is obvious that the implications of Candler's great success — surely clear to anyone by 1900 — were not lost on Bradham; by 1902 he had abandoned the running of his drugstore to someone else and had formed The Pepsi-Cola Company, a North Carolina corporation. He registered the name "Pepsi-Cola" as a trademark in early 1903.

Bradham realized that a great part of Candler's success was directly attributable to advertising, so he began advertising his drink in February, 1903, some four months before the trademark registration process was formally completed. The New Bern *Journal* of February 25, 1903, with a front page filled with such epochal news as the arrival in town of Dr. J. P. Lewis of New York City, and the blowing out of a flue on Engine No. 17 on the A & NC freight No. 2, indexed, as was its custom, the new advertisements of the day. Along with "Lost . . . On the Academy Green a small open face gold watch. The person finding same will be amply paid by returning it to me. — J. J. Baxter" and "Rooms for rent . . . Three desirable rooms for rent at 34 Hancock Street. No one with children need apply," there was Pepsi-Cola. The stylized trademark script (Bradham wisely avoided unnecessary entanglement with Coca-Cola by limiting his script to the "P" and "C" and block-lettering the rest) contained the 5¢ price in the bottom loop of the "C," the word "Drink" in the backward-flowing top of the "C," and "Delicious-Healthful" in a long band which connected the bottom of the "P" and the bottom of the "C." He proclaimed the drink "Exhilarating, Invigorating," claimed that it "Aids Digestion" and said it could be purchased "At Soda Fountains."

It was probably an effective ad—it certainly leapt out of the unremitting grey of the front page—but it was only one column wide and two inches deep. Its size was symbolic of Bradham's problem: in 1903 he spent $1,888.78 on advertising and sold 7,968 gallons of syrup. The Coca-Cola Company spent $207,008.29 on advertising that year, and sold 881,423 gallons of syrup. Bradham was undaunted by his powerful competitor, and by 1907 he was selling 104,000 gallons of syrup, and had established a network of 40 bottling plants.

Bradham, like everyone else in the business, chased Coca-Cola by using the same advertising methods which had worked so well for Coke. Perhaps he was an acute mimic, or perhaps because he was marketing a cola drink, but whatever the reason, his advertising, whether in the form of metal serving and change trays (page 140) or print, was remarkably like that which was prepared for Coca-Cola. In print, where Coca-Cola had been endorsed by Ty Cobb or Walter Johnson or George Stallings (the manager of the 1914 "miracle" Boston Braves), Pepsi in 1909 had its own testimonial:

"Here's what Barney Oldfield, the famous automobile racing driver, says about Pepsi-Cola:

"'I enjoy Pepsi-Cola first rate. It's a bully drink—refreshing, invigorating, a fine bracer before a race, and a splendid restorer afterwards.'

"Pepsi-Cola is the Original Pure Food Drink—guaranteed under the U.S. Gov't Serial No. 3813. At all soda fountains, 5¢ a glass—at your grocer's, 5¢ a bottle. Beware of imitations."

In 1907 Coca-Cola "had come to the modern business man". Pepsi followed two years later:

"You can work better in warm weather by drinking delicious Pepsi-Cola during business hours. Wonderfully refreshing—overcomes fatigue and exhaustion. Keep it in the office and it will keep you fit for work. Guaranteed under the Pure Food Law. At all fountains and in bottles."

Bradham probably reached the peak of his success at the end of 1915. He had already erected a new headquarters building for the company, a source of great pride for him (to keep this accomplishment in perspective, New Bern wasn't New York, where there was a building built for Coca-Cola and neither was it Atlanta). Bradham was, however, ready to lay siege to Coca-Cola in its home grounds, a plan which he announced with a full page ad in the October 5, 1915, *National Bottlers' Gazette:*

"Pepsi-Cola is now ready to invade Georgia, Florida, Mississippi and Louisiana.

"We offer bottling privileges and exclusive territory in these five states to bottlers who are prepared to take hold of a 'live,' liberal-profit proposition and work it to the same success that has met the efforts of hundreds of bottlers in North and South Carolina and Virginia.

"Every Pepsi-Cola bottler in these States is reaping wonderful profits with an ever-increasing production. Look at these examples:

Production in Gallons	1912	1913	1914	1915 (est.)
Greensboro, N.C.	3096	7447	12760	15000
Winston-Salem, N.C.	5041	8934	12243	18000
Suffolk, Va.	1010	1368	1743	3000
Greenville, N.C.	451	1540	2307	4000

"Write to any of the Pepsi-Cola Bottling Companies in these towns, or in any of a hundred others, such as: Norfolk, Charlottesville, Lynchburg or Danville, Va.; or Kingston, Tarboro, Washington, Wilson and Raleigh, N.C.; or Darlington, Columbia, Charleston and Georgetown, S.C., and find out what *they* think of the Pepsi-Cola proposition.

"We know of no reason why wide-awake bottlers can't make just as great profits from Pepsi-Cola in the new territory as these bottlers have in theirs.

"Pepsi-Cola is a drink with a 'punch'—it has won a recognized place through its wonderful flavor and after-effect, and its popularity is constantly growing.

"And we know that a wide-awake bottler gets such cooperation with this inimitable product that he *just can't help making a success of his business.*

"Are *you* the wide-awake bottler of your district?

"Write us today if you want to get in on the ground floor.

"/s/ C. D. Bradham, President."

It was the last of Bradham's brave talk, for he was to be one of the serious casualties of the war. After sustaining the decline in sales occasioned by rationing of sugar, he was blitzed by the post-war sugar price inflation. As the price soared, Bradham, like everyone else in the soft drink business, was faced with the unhappy choice of either buying at inflated prices as a hedge against further price increases (even though all possibility of profitability was destroyed), or not buying and waiting for the price to drop. If the price didn't drop far enough fast enough, not buying meant simply not having a business. With the price around 22¢ a pound in May, 1920, Bradham bought. He was brilliant in doing so, for the price soared even further to 26¢. But in December he wasn't so smart, for the price broke suddenly, plummeting all the way to 3¢ a pound.

When a man sits with a warehouse full of 22¢ sugar in a 3¢ market, he inevitably is sitting with corporate books that are written in blood-red ink. The Pepsi-Cola Company lost $150,000 in 1920, which, after the lost volume of the war years, left the company without much capital. Bradham tried to raise some by borrowing, but was unsuccessful. Then he tried to sell farm lands, which the company had been acquiring, in return for its stock, but land was as cheap as sugar; Bradham's holdings were worth far less on the open market than they were on the company books. Finally, Bradham tried to sell more stock, and failed in that. By 1922 the company showed assets of some $53,000 and liabilities of nearly $250,000.

The only hope for Bradham was in a complete reorganization, which the company attempted with the help of a Wall Street firm, R. C. Megargel & Company. The plan was for a new corporation to be formed in Delaware, with its shares to be exchanged for shares in the old company. Creditors were to be paid off with bonds, and the Megargel company was to have an option to buy a huge chunk of stock. The success of the plan, of course, depended on getting the public to buy stock in the new corporation, something which the public resisted with the same fervor it had shown toward the last stock offering of the North Carolina company. The scheme collapsed, and the trademark and business of the old company were never formally transferred to the new, which expired in 1925. The old company went under much sooner. It was ruled bankrupt in Federal Court in 1923, and a few months later its assets were sold to a North Carolina holding company, formed for the express purpose of making the purchase by creditors of Pepsi-Cola who wanted to consolidate their misery. The holding company paid $30,000 so that the creditors could have the privilege of quietly picking over the sugar-bleached bones of The Pepsi-Cola Company.

The sugar price break, had, to be certain, posed great problems for the new owners of Pepsi's greatest competition.

CHAPTER 8

Ernest Woodruff, head of the group which bought out the Candlers, was from all accounts, a crusty, gruff, enormously shrewd promoter, whose favorite business practice was gathering small companies and turning them into one larger company which would be capitalized for more than the sum of its parts, with Woodruff taking a cut of the magic profit he had created. He had, in this manner, put together Atlantic Ice & Coal, Continental Gin, Atlantic Steel, and The Trust Company of Georgia. At first glance, his purchase of Coca-Cola seemed to have been made as just another good business deal. Impressive as the sales growth of Coca-Cola had been, it was still concentrated in the South, and Woodruff must have banked on similar growth in the other parts of the country.

You do not have to be a financial Lenny Bernstein to whistle the melody that Woodruff and his associates had composed. Immediately after gaining control of the company, Woodruff reconstituted it as a Delaware corporation, and had the corporation issue 500,000 new shares of common stock, which he, his associates, and his bank bought at $5 a share. (Recall, as Woodruff surely must have, that Asa Candler's original 500-plus shares were worth nearly $50,000 each when the Candlers sold.) Unfortunately, Woodruff's hope for soaring prices for his stock depended, at the very least, on maintenance of the sales growth of the company. But in the years following the purchase, Coca-Cola sales declined.

The problem originated with the sugar crisis, and affected the relationship between the Company and the bottlers of Coke. By 1917, over 1,000 bottling franchises had been granted (a number which would not materially change — at least, domestically — over the next 50 years). Though bottle sales still represented a minority of total syrup sales, a great deal of corporate energy was expended on the bottler/sugar problem.

Given the catastrophic price of sugar, the most insoluble difficulty Atlanta faced was the written contracts that tied Atlanta with the parent bottlers. The Coca-Cola Company was committed to a syrup price; so were the parent bottlers in their relationships with the bottlers. But Atlanta could not hold to its price if it had to put twenty- or twenty-two cent sugar into the syrup. It had, however, precious little leverage with which to force the bottlers to accept a higher price. Each bottler held his franchise in perpetuity, dealt with Atlanta through the parent bottler middleman, and in most cases had been associated with the bottling of Coke for a comparatively short time, which made for less loyalty to the drink than would later be the norm. The Coca-Cola Company could punish the bottlers only by cutting the flow of syrup entirely, an act which would have amounted to a suicide pact of epic proportions.

Atlanta moved to protect itself in two ways, using (it should come as no great tactical surprise) the old carrot-and-stick approach. The stick was wielded, as sticks generally are in corporate affairs, by the legal department of The Coca-Cola Company, which filed suit challenging the lifetime contracts that bound the bottlers to Coca-Cola (or, more to the point of it, bound Coca-Cola to obstinate bottlers). The carrot took the unlikely form of a hulking Georgian named Harrison Jones, an executive of The Coca-Cola Company, who stood before a bottlers' convention and delivered what is remembered as the Southern precursor to Churchill's later war orations. Jones eloquently pointed out the stark fact that cooperation was needed in eating the sugar losses if one or another branch of the business was not to swallow them whole and expire. Let us work together, he cried, let us meet this adversity together. The oratory had great effect; so did the threatened suit, even though experts would later say that the bottlers probably would have won. The bottlers and the company came to an understanding — that the bottlers would pay the already agreed-upon price for the syrup, but that the bottlers would share with the Company the cost of sugar above the usual market price, and the lawsuit was dropped.

This great effort to save the Company would have been rendered pointless, of course, if the legal battle with The Koke Company of America was lost. But, however much The Coca-Cola Company seemed to have damaged its own case by its advertising insistence on use of the full brand name, it had a formidable weapon in a lawyer named Harold Hirsch. Hirsch was probably the greatest expert in trademark law of the day. Nor did he lack for practical experience: he was in court, representing Coca-Cola, with a frequency which today would stagger even the most hardened Perry Mason habitué. Company officials would later concede privately that Hirsch's knowledge and reputation had enabled him to win cases for Coca-Cola, which he should have lost. But the Company was riding a remarkable legal winning streak. It had been vindicated in Chattanooga. It had won a host of trademark cases. It had even won a suit it had filed against the government, around the turn of the century — a suit which had asked for the return of taxes levied on Coca-Cola as a medicinal item. That case was tried only a few years after Candler had shifted the focus of Coca-Cola advertising from the pharmacists' counter to the soda fountain. Seemingly, the government's defense could have rested on clippings of Coca-Cola advertisements. The jury, however, ruled for Coca-Cola.

Coke v Koke went to the Supreme Court, which not only found for Coca-Cola, but handed down a decision written by Oliver Wendell Holmes, containing a line that has since been engraved on the heart of every loyal Company executive, describing the drink as "a single thing coming from a single source and well known to the community."

There was one other major factor in the postwar sales decline: the executive shakeup which had taken place when Woodruff and his associates had bought the Company. Candler's son Howard resigned the presidency, to be replaced by Candler's nephew, the original go-getter of the Company, Sam Dobbs. There is evidence though that Dobbs, or rather Dobbs as a reflection of corporate thinking, was uncertain about who should be drinking Coca-Cola.

Obviously, the thinking then as now was that *everyone* should be drinking Coke. Today, dense concentrations of people in urban areas, coupled with the media's penetration into everyone's life—notably through radio and television—has produced a situation in which a company can reasonably decide to try and reach an enormous number of people with a message about its product. In 1919 and 1920, however, decisions still had to be made about which segment of the American public was to be exposed to a Coke sales blitz.

Dobbs and The Coca-Cola Company decided to focus their efforts on exactly the wrong group. In 1920, the Company produced a handsome booklet, describing that year's advertising sales campaign and reproducing the ads which would run in newspapers and magazines. The booklet opened with a suitably exhortatory message from Sam Dobbs to the salesmen: "Therefore, cultivate the dealer—the man behind the counter—the ten-dollar-a-week clerk. Make him your ally; become his; give him to feel that you are interested in him. Tomorrow he may be the owner of his own store." Then it ran through eight pages, dispensing balm to the faint-hearted by showing through various simple charts and graphs just how great the soft-drink industry was. The final chart, for example, illustrated the fact that the soft-drink business required less horsepower to manufacture a given amount of merchandise—430 horsepower, if you're interested, for each $1,000,000 of production, as against 918 horsepower needed to manufacture that amount in other forms of industry.

After finishing with that bit of inspired silliness (silly only because it was the sort of thing which might have been produced to restore the sagging spirits of investors in Coca-Cola stock, or lure new investors), the reader turned the page to be greeted with the headline, "Who Produces the Dollar?" For the salesmen, that was more like it. Whoever produced the dollar could presumably be persuaded to part with one-twentieth of it for a glass of Coke. Underneath the headline, a bold pie chart showed that the person who produced most of the dollars, 70 percent of them, in fact was—oops! —the farmer.

There actually was one person responsible for coming up with the magic figure of 70 percent. Taking the fall was F. O. Watts, the President of the First National Bank of St. Louis, who wrote, "'I have realized for a long while that the basic wealth of our nation was founded in soil production, but the real force of it was brought home to me the other day when, by analysis, I found that about 70 percent of every dollar we handle in the bank here is a *farm dollar* [emphasis in the original], having its origin in farm production.'" Thus pointed down the garden path, the Company was ready to proceed with a gallop. "Inasmuch as such a percentage of our new money is found in the hands of the farmer, is he not with his $24,000,000,000 annual income worth cultivating? Nor should the fact be overlooked that this harvest of spending money is derived from his total aggregate investment of $70,000,000,000. This is not millions, but 70 billions of dollars. Not only does he with his family ride to town oftener than formerly, but in their 2,750,000 automobiles these families are enabled to attend more functions than heretofore; and they want the best of everything — are going to get it — and they are ready to pay for it."

If the Company had had the benefit of being able to wait for the Cagney movies of the '30s, with the montage shots of boys going off to war from the farms, and then returning to newly-burgeoning cities, it might have avoided betting its sales chips on what was to be a dwindling segment of the population. Unfortunately, all the Company had to go on was Watts, and another stunning bit of misdirected information, which was reproduced (natch) in the booklet — the Provost Marshal General's Draft Classification of Industrial Workers from World War I. The breakdown of the American labor force in 1917 was:

Farmers and Farm Laborers	13,843,518
Bankers, Brokers, Insurance, Real Estate, Salesmen, Clerks, etc.	4,708,908
Barbers, Bartenders, Cooks, Waiters, Servants, etc.	4,208,862
Laborers	4,053,385
Carpenters, Painters, Plasterers, Plumbers, Blacksmiths, Machinists, etc.	2,878,792
Journalists, Lawyers, Doctors, Actors, etc.	2,202,609

Telegraph, Telephone, Railroad	1,533,934
Electric Railways, Cab Drivers, Boatmen, Highways	1,297,132
Brooms, Brushes, Cigars, Straw Factories, etc.	1,254,361
Mines, Quarries, Wells	926,932
Textile Industries	919,800
Leather and Lumber	885,731
Clothing Factories	754,062
Chemicals, Fertilizer, etc.	425,900
Steel Mills	373,701
Metal Ware	268,537

Categories which either had too few people to be worried about on the chart, or were simply considered unimportant no matter how many employed, were Public Administration, and Agricultural Implements, Autos, Wagons, Boats, etc.

A clear call to battle was derived from close study of these charts: "The farmers are there and so are their families and they have a thirst to quench as the result of their long hours of hard labor. Compare the number of farmers with the number of individuals in any other three classifications and then remember that these farmers have large and growing families who not only yearn for the best, but have the money to pay for it."

Sales of Coca-Cola slid downward. Whether that slide was greater or less than the lessening of the farm labor force of the period would seem to be a good subject for a Ph.D. dissertation at the Harvard Business School. As sales declined, the magic properties of Woodruff's stock almost disappeared. For a time, The Trust Company of Georgia was reduced to trying to unload its shares along with mortgage loans it was granting, a bit of arm-twisting which turned out well for the twistees, as the value of those $5 shares soared to $900 (taking into account splits), with $475 in dividends paid, by the end of World War II.

The man who made this turnabout possible was a 33-year-old executive vice president of the White Motor Company in Cleveland in 1923. In the spring of that year, the board of directors of Coca-Cola, Ernest Woodruff abstaining, elected this fellow to the Company presidency; he was Ernest Woodruff's son, Robert.

The elder Woodruff had raised his son, in that creaky phrase, to know the value of a dollar. He did it by setting an example. For instance, having purchased some $2,000,000 in bonds in Cleveland, the elder Woodruff learned that the cost of having the bonds shipped to Atlanta was $200. Instead of paying this relatively small sum, he strapped the bonds to himself and his secretary, and the two gentlemen locked themselves in their train compartment for the journey home. Robert Woodruff was later to say that "every time those two sat down, they crackled like diplomas."

While Robert Woodruff would be raised with advantages which could only be the result of extreme wealth (at one point he took a 10,000-mile trip around the country in a private railroad car belonging to one of his father's friends), he was never pampered. For example, he was given a fifty-cent-a-week allowance to buy feed for the pony he rode to school. Asa Candler being his Sunday School teacher, Robert soon found that the Candler-owned Coca-Cola stables were near his school. So he struck up a friendship with the stableman, which resulted in his pony being stabled and fed for free, leaving him with a clear profit of fifty cents a week.

Later, Robert quit college, over his father's strenuous objections, to go to work. In fact, having quit school, he *had* to go to work, since his father would not honor his college debts. Robert started as a laborer in a foundry, and then landed a job with a fire extinguisher company, where he became a salesman, such a good salesman that his father offered him a job at Atlantic Ice & Coal for $150 a month. Robert wanted to get married, so he took the job, and almost immediately outraged his father by purchasing, without prior consultation or authorization, a fleet of White trucks to replace the firm's horse-drawn wagons. The deal so angered the elder Woodruff, who evidently was inclined to believe that automobiles were a passing fad, that he summarily fired his son, who was immediately hired by Walter White of the truck company. White did not want the young man to work for anyone else, explaining later, "I thought I had a sucker when I got hold of that youngster and started selling him trucks. I ended up with a deal in which my profit wouldn't have bought the shirt on my back that I almost lost."

Robert Woodruff quickly rose from salesman to an executive position in the White home office, where he soon was named a vice president (in those days vice presidents were not as common in corporate affairs as they are today). He was, and is, an extremely quiet, shy man, who believed in listening to all sides of a question before coming to an executive decision. (A lot of people holding important positions like to say that they weigh all the alternatives, listen to all the facts, before reaching conclusions—the most obvious example being Richard M. Nixon. In practice certain sides of a question are given short shrift, if examined at all. Woodruff, however, is known for hearing out even those arguments which he would detest before, during, and after consideration.)

When he got to Atlanta, one of the people Woodruff listened to most closely was a young ex-newspaperman named Archie Lee, who worked on the Coca-Cola account at the D'Arcy advertising agency. Together, Woodruff and Lee were to create some of the best advertising ever done for Coca-Cola or any other product, and were to draw a picture of America which has lasted (if only in vivid memory) until today.

POP.

CHAPTER 9

Archie Lee came out of Monroe, North Carolina, eager to make a reputation in the world. Like many other Southern boys, he envisioned making his mark by writing, and planned to start with journalism.*

By 1917 Lee was working as a newspaperman in Atlanta. His career can best be traced by the letters he wrote home:

April 5, 1917

My dear Mama:

It seems to me that it has almost come about in the affairs of this nation and the world at large that it doesn't matter much anyway what an individual thinks and feels. Those of us who have clung to a philosophy of individualism have been swept by currents of millions of human beings into an entirely new world . . .

. . . the full force of this great change is just now breaking upon this country. I have talked with a number of prominent men recently and they say that the activities of the government within the next several months will make this a changed country.

The old problems of car shortages, money panics, labor strikes and the like will be no more. We are going to raise an army and

---

*The top ranks of the best newspapers over the past thirty years or so have been filled with Southerners who came from small towns; this has been most noticeable at the New York Times.

enlarge our navy in a way that will startle our friends as well as our enemies . . . Our government is changing in fact if not in name. What we have called our personal liberty and individual freedom are things of the past. Everything and everybody is being mobilized into a strong government that has a vision of transcending wealth and power.

All of our officials and leaders are coating the dose we all must take with finely spun theories of ideals. They talk about the dethronement of kings and a new freedom of the people. Such talk, to me, harks back to the pratings of the Abolitionists of New England of Civil War days. They were going to free the negro and elevate him to liberty and light. The negro is the same today as he was 50 years ago . . .

***The world will be changed all right; but it won't be the end of wars. This country will be more warlike than ever before. It will develop undreamed-of strength. And it will remain in a state of preparedness to meet the menace of Japan and other ambitious nations. The fear of Japan, in fact, is having much to do with the present movement. We must let them know that we are strong and unafraid.

The time may come when the rest of the world will look upon our ambitions and strength as a menace to them. When there are great fortunes to be gained by imposing on weaker peoples, you can't stop men. The curse of money is upon the world . . .

***I want to do something really worthwhile. I would die happy if it should be just one recognized and lasting thing.

The means I have adopted is writing. I will strive on through the years with the earnest hope that at last my ambition may be realized . . .

***I have not yet had my triumph in life. My patience with it all is strained. I have more sympathy with Dean Swift and Dr. Samuel Johnson than with Browning and Tennyson. That attitude in itself may bring me the place and recognition I crave. A man who can see life in its true colors and describe it in words can gain fortune and fame.

Fortune and fame! They make a lot of difference.

I can never be happy as a commonplace man. A home and the love of a woman are not enough. I sometimes suspect that I have let them slip through my fingers in keeping my eye fixed on the other reward.

The only real love I bear is to you all at home.
I would like to do something worthwhile for your sake as much as for my own.

Your loving son,

Archie Lee

By 1920, Lee was working for the D'Arcy Advertising Agency in St. Louis. For all his philosophical speculations on business, he knew a good thing when he saw it:

March 13, 1920

My dear Papa:

When I was home last you told me that if I saw a good investment you would let me have $1,000. I know one that I am anxious to take advantage of—Coca-Cola stock that is selling low at the present time but which, I have assurance, is certain to rise when warm weather sets in. I am not contemplating speculation. I would buy the stock outright and put it away as a permanent investment. [One which would be worth a cool $180,000 by 1945, with $95,000 more having been paid on it in dividends over the years.]

I would not have you make any sacrifice to do this for me. I am writing you my desires solely because you made the offer. The investment is absolutely safe and there is a big chance that it will net a good profit, perhaps leading the way to a real fortune.

I am writing five accounts, the total expenditures on which will exceed $500,000 during the year. In addition to that, I do a good deal of the Coca-Cola work, and The Coca-Cola Company spends more than the five others combined. It is hard work, giving a different dress to many stories about the same thing. The company is giving me ample opportunity to show my capacity, and I feel sure that the efforts I am putting forth will bear abundant fruit.

Devotedly,

Archie Lee

A year later, Lee was the comer in the D'Arcy office. He was handling more and more of the work for Coca-Cola.

March 8, 1921

My dear Papa:

***When we came back from Atlanta Christmas, we brought along Candler Dobbs, the son of the Mr. Dobbs who was president of The Coca-Cola Company. He is 24 but very young for his age. Although his father is rich, he is making the son live on his income. This boy comes to me with all his troubles, his love affairs and everything else. He is really funny and interesting.

He worries Mr. D'Arcy nearly to death, trying to see him many times every day. Mr. D'Arcy has put it up to me to straighten him out as to how he should conduct himself around the office. It is not an easy job. The boy is very ambitious to get ahead, but he doesn't know how to do anything but clerical work, and he doesn't want to do that. It will be interesting to watch and see how his case works out. . . .

I get a mild shock every now and then when I think how the years are flying and how my life has been changing. Isn't it wonderful just to live and to observe. Somehow you sense a great purpose back of it all.

I have been doing the best work I have ever done in my life. I have written the entire Coca-Cola campaign for this year and am getting closer and closer to D'Arcy all the time. I feel confident that my reward will not be inconsiderable.***

Devotedly,

Archie

Over the next months Lee learned more and more about the kind of work that goes into preparing a large advertising campaign, but what was more important, he was always watching the men with whom he did business, measuring the elements which went into success, noting those which led to failure.

October 29, 1921

My dear Papa:

***Mr. D'Arcy was with me in Atlanta and we had a very successful conference with The Coca-Cola Company's officials. They approved a good part of next year's Coca-Cola advertising. I wish I could show you the array of stuff we took down. In no other way than in seeing a comprehensive campaign can you visualize the work of an advertising agency in handling a big account. We had prepared more than fifty pieces of copy, most of the pieces in colors. Mr. Candler [by this time Dobbs was out as President, replaced by Charles Howard Candler] said it was the best material that had ever been presented to them. That made me feel proud because I had a big part in preparing it.

But one accomplishment is not a cause for rest. It but opens the way to greater effort.***

"There is no expedient to which a man will not resort to avoid the real labor of thinking."

That quotation from the writings of Sir Joshua Reynolds, hangs upon the wall of the private office of Thomas A. Edison.

To me, it expressed what an important thing in the affairs of the world thinking is. Lack of it is the cause of most business troubles. I have seen so many business men afflicted with the arrogance of ignorance. Because they say a thing they insist it is right. We call them narrow and foolish. The trouble is they are lazy—they are dodging the work of thinking out the facts and the truth. Being too lazy to think is the cause of religious prejudice—the cause of Republican administrations, threatened railroad strikes, prohibition, bad roads and divorces. People have plenty of ability to act intelligently if they would only think.

But thinking is exacting work. Doing it is humbling—we can glimpse so much beyond our grasp. But it builds the mind, and the mind, unlike the body, will never cease growing if it is properly cultivated.***

Much love,

Archie

Eight months later, Lee was to renew an acquaintance he had made years before, with a man who was always involved with his own philosophical introspection, and who measured up to every standard Lee set for a businessman: Robert Woodruff.

July 7, 1922

My dear Mama:

***I got to my office this morning just five minutes before I began writing this letter—returning from three days in Cleveland. Several of us have been up going over the White plant. It is a marvelous institution with some 6,000 employees. They do most of their business with the greatest concerns in the country, the old companies, express companies, etc. The business was founded by an old New England family, the Whites. They are unusually fine people, highly educated, cultured and very rich. We got the business through a combination of circumstances. A fellow about my age and the son of a prominent banker in Atlanta, a fellow I met when I first went to Atlanta years ago, started selling White trucks about the time I went to work on the newspaper in Atlanta. He did remarkably well, and after the war he was taken to Cleveland and soon became General Manager of The White Company. In the meantime, The Coca-Cola Company was sold, and in time this fellow's father came into control of The Coca-Cola Company. He wanted his son back in Atlanta. Although he [Robert] was making lots of money in Cleveland, he went back to Atlanta a few months ago as president of The Coca-Cola Company. This man is Robert Woodruff. Through him we came to know the officers of The White Company, and now we have the advertising of The White Company as well as that of Coca-Cola.

Altogether we represent about 30 different manufacturers, but these two stand out as the biggest successes. Mr. D'Arcy himself has direction of these two accounts and I am his first aide in doing the thinking and the writing. For example, after the conference in Cleveland, he left for Maine to be with his family for a week, and I am back here to get the advertising into shape for a conference with him and then its presentation to The White Company.

I have gone into some detail to try and give you an idea of my work. Of course I work on the advertising of other products, but these two things demand more brains and bring the largest returns. Sometimes I mentally detach myself from the whole thing, and I almost tremble at what I assume I am capable of doing. The work demands the best thought of its kind that can be done. If someone else could show we were not doing the work well, we would lose the business. We are in competition with the best brains in America. I am proud to say that our agency ranks as one of the best in the United States.

Here is big opportunity. I have not arrived at this opportunity except by the hardest kind of work and overcoming the keenest sort of competition. It should mean that I should make more and more money. For the first time I can say that I am on a firm footing with a number of men with lots of money and great business ability. The way to make money, of course, is to get in with people who have broad visions and are making it in large quantities. They need brains. Much brains goes to waste because of a lack of this sort of contact. You see I have attained something of that for which I hoped when a good many years ago I swallowed the lump in my throat and moved away from home. How well I can capitalize on this opportunity depends wholly on me. Thanks to you and papa, I have a mind capable of growing and expanding from year to year, an early education and a degree of culture which enables me to meet important people without self-consciousness, a free tongue to talk and a certain facility, born of a determination to do one thing well, at writing. It all goes back to home—to you and papa and the life and training of childhood, where springs of aspiration in my heart first were tapped. I cite these things because I know it is a lack of them and failure to understand them that cause men to fail.

Don't get from this that I think I am sitting on top of the world. What I mean is that I have climbed up to a plane of opportunity. I am making a reputation in advertising. And often as we work, if we work well, we build better than we know, and I feel more hopeful and more optimistic about what I should accomplish than ever before in my life. No small part of this is due to Mr. D'Arcy's confidence in me and in my ability.

Devotedly,

Archie

Lee's greatest ability was that of refining and polishing the advertising concept which had remained remarkably constant since 1886. Since the drinking of Coca-Cola was a matter of impulse, meant to be as casual as possible on the part of the customer, the advertising had to be, on the one hand, obtrusive enough so as constantly to remind the potential customer that that point in time could be made more pleasurable by ingesting a Coke. On the other hand, truly obtrusive advertising — the kind of jackhammer idiocy that today is associated with various pain relievers and soaps —would make the drinking of a Coke less a pleasant act, engaged in naturally, than one that resulted from the bludgeon. Metaphorically speaking, it would be the difference between seduction and rape.

The seductiveness in the advertising was accomplished by showing extremely pleasant scenes meant to represent everyday life—scenes in which people were buying, transporting, drinking or otherwise involved with Coca-Cola. Everyday life, as first shown by the ads for Coke, consisted exclusively of good-looking women; Asa Candler had discovered that good-looking women were as beneficial to sales as the magic properties of the "Erythroxylon Coca Plant." In the 1970s, when the showing of good-looking women in advertisements is regarded as degrading by feminists and equated, not without reason, with advocacy of instant consummation of the sexual act, any sexual act, it is difficult to understand how reasonable this idea was in 1887. Candler's theory was that the women in his ads should be in their mid- to late-20s, an age, he figured, that younger people aspired to because of the charm connected with it, and an age which older people like to remember. Candler also believed that the women portrayed were attractive not only to men, but also to women, who could see in the pictures things to emulate or criticize.

The only time that the ads engendered any real criticism came when the Western Coca-Cola Bottling Company, located in Chicago, decided to create its own advertising: a serving tray, which showed a woman nude to the waist, clutching a bottle of Coca-Cola; and a couple of trade cards and posters in the same general vein. It was pretty racy stuff for 1908, all right; and it is said that Candler viewed the effort with mixed emotions. He was legally powerless to stop them (contracts limiting bottlers to ads prepared by The Coca-Cola Company wouldn't be negotiated for a number of years). And while he thought that the nudity was going a *leetle* bit too far, what really got his dander up was the fact that the ads touted Coke as a wonderful mixer for liquor. Asa was a teetotaler. Still, wasn't it selling Coke?

But showing pretty girls, or everyday life (stylized and idealized, to be sure), of themselves would not have been enough to make the advertising memorable. There was also the matter of graphic style. Ads for Coke, like the rest of American commerical art, had evolved from the formal and static art, produced by anonymous artists for lithographers in the early days of the century, to the free-flowing illustrative styles, produced by well-known artists for use in the large-circulation slick magazines in the '20s and later. (It is not unlikely that this shift in style, comparable in many ways to the shift in fine art from the French Academy style of the mid-1800s to the Impressionists of the 1860s and later, was due in large part to the improvement in printing techniques, which allowed for subtler use of color without the risk of botched printing.)

As the graphic quality of the art in the ads changed (compare the lady frozen on the 1904 metal tray [page 139] with the woman in the bathing suit on the 1932 serving tray [page 150], who looks as though she is about to get up and walk toward you), Lee and his compatriots at D'Arcy began to use less and less text to get their message across. In the 'teens they were writing long, steamy odes to Coca-Cola. ("Fresh, with the fragrance of Springtime— Sweet, with the ripe fruits of Summer—Red, with the blushes of Autumn—Chilled, with the white snows of Winter. The delicious gift of all seasons—the refreshing drink of the year.") By the 1920s, they were down to a few words, "It Had to be Good to Get Where It Is." (The most famous slogan of them all, "The Pause That Refreshes," came out of a Saturday afternoon brainstorming session at the ad agency. Though many of the participants at that meeting subsequently claimed authorship of the line, it appears from the accounts of less-biased observers that it was Archie Lee himself who melded the familiar—to Coke advertising, anyway—words, "Refreshing" and "Pause" into the final slogan.)

An interesting sidelight to the art that D'Arcy was so brilliantly producing was the fact that the people at the agency were incapable of describing what it was they were up to. In 1925 someone at the agency decided that it would be beneficial for the agency to have an "analysis" of the advertising it had produced for Coke during the previous decade. Some researchers dug out all the advertising D'Arcy had on file and catalogued it on several mammoth sheets of paper. The descriptions of what was termed "art appeal" in the ads are illuminating, mostly for their lack of illumination. The 1916 piece showing the artist painting the calendar girl (page 73), for example, was supposed to have had an "art appeal" of "Charming youth and beauty." Got that? Among the other categories of "art appeal" were "fresh wholesome youth, charming youth-purity, youthful freshness, vigorous youth, freshness of youth and spring, natural wholesomeness, natural refreshment, thirst, wholesome youth, American youth, romantic youth."

Ironically enough, what such artists as Fred Mizen, Hayden Hayden, Haddon Sundblom, Norman Rockwell, and N. C. Wyeth, to name a few, were doing for D'Arcy was exactly what such artists as Dorothea Lange, Walker Evans, Ben Shahn, and others were to do with camera for the Farm Security Administration during the '30s—that is, capture the spirit of America. And where neither Archie Lee nor anyone else at D'Arcy was formally to write down what it was that the agency was up to, Roy Stryker, who headed the photographic section of the FSA, drew up an incredibly detailed assignment memo for his photographers sometime in 1936, which included a subsection called "American Habit." Listed in this section were "Small Town: Main Street; Courthouse square; Ice Cream parlor; R.R. station-watching the train 'go through'; Sitting on the front porch; Women visiting from porch to street; Cutting the lawn; Watering the lawn; Eating ice cream cones; Waiting for the bus; In the phone booth; Hanging out washing in back yard; Women talking over back fence; Soda counter-high school kids." As if the parallel with the D'Arcy artists weren't clear enough, consider another category, "Eating: Ice cream cones; Corn on the cob; Watermelon-Southern towns; Picnics; Barbeques; Hot dogs-Cokes in bottles."

In all the memo, only two products are mentioned by brand name — Good Humor, and Coca-Cola (which was also listed as a possible photographic subject in the category of scenes at gas stations). It is probable that somewhere in the Library of Congress, there are on file photographs by Walker Evans or John Vachon or Russell Lee or Dorothea Lange which make exactly the point that Archie Lee was making: central to the American experience was the act of drinking Coca-Cola.

CHAPTER 10

A note about the following illustrations:

There are dozens more items that might have been included in this book. A complete catalog is another undertaking altogether—for a less discriminating or more thorough collector than the author of this volume. In selecting the most interesting items, and those best reproduced, we eliminated, among other wonderful things, the photo of Clark Gable and Jean Harlow posing for Coke.

The 1937 tray.

The pause that refreshes
FRANCES DEE
and
GENE RAYMOND
on Malibu Beach

In the early
'30s, Coke was
heavily
promoted
by film stars.
Considering
that Joan
Crawford has
since become
identified with
Pepsi, it is
doubtful that
she kept
pictures such as
this one in her
scrapbooks.
Whoever
designed
Garbo's suit
should have
been shot.

Pocket mirrors, which were free or 5¢, today sell for $100 and up. Upper left was issued in 1912; upper right c. 1906; lower left, from 1917; lower right, 1920.

This small pendant showed the calendar girl from 1908. The card on the table had the then-current slogan for Coke: Good to the last drop.

There is no evidence that this photo was used for promotional display. It shows young Norman Rockwell "working" on the painting used for the 1931 tray. The clear difference between model and painting was artistic license. Too bad, however, that Rockwell took a terrific Airedale and made it into a mutt.

The Rockwell
tray. This
scene, known as
"Tom Sawyer,"
was also used
for the 1931
calendar.
Rockwell
also did a
fishing boy for
the 1932
calendar
(known as
Huckleberry
Finn, what
else?), and
another young
fisherman for
the 1935
calendar.

CHAPTER 11

Where Asa Candler's great merchandising idea had come from not wanting to wait until someone got sick for him to be a potential customer, Woodruff's was in not wanting to wait until someone got thirsty. Moreover, Woodruff was shrewd enough to know that there is a fair amount of manipulation involved in all human interchange; and that there was a fair amount involved in getting Coca-Cola into the gullets of Americans.

The manipulation in the case of Coke — the manipulation in a case of Coke, if you will — came in finding out just what it was that caused a person to drink something. This may sound preposterous, but consider how much liquid you drink because of genuine thirst — the kind you are dying of — and how much you drink because of ingrained social patterns, and how much when you get right into it, of what you might at first consider *gen-u-ine* thirst, of which you are dying, is not in fact the product of some subtle, learned response. Some of the subtle responses have been learned from The Coca-Cola Company, which began in the '20s to conduct market research and market psychology studies, interviewing millions of people to find out why they drank, and especially, why they drank soft drinks. Armed with this mass of data, the Company was in a position to try and push the right psychological buttons to keep Coke flowing.

Once the decision had been made as to which responses to cultivate with advertising (however imperfect D'Arcy's descriptions of how this was to be done), the crucial step was in getting the ads to the people. While the sheer amount of money spent might lead you to conclude that the tactic behind the advertising of Coke was simply in putting those ads everywhere, wall to wall to wall, this is and was not ever quite the case. The Coca-Cola Company was the first major corporation to chart automobile traffic flow so that billboards and signs could be placed on the most heavily travelled streets. Though you may sourly note that this idea has led to a situation where you often can't see the billboards for the billboards, it was an idea which was first copied by municipal and state governments, which set their traffic or road departments to work following the model provided by the guys who were selling Coke.

All of this had contributed to syrup sales of 26.9 million gallons in 1929. The nation was floating in Coke; The Coca-Cola Company was floating in profits. Of course, the nationwide sales push of Coke had not been hurt by the inescapable fact that many thirsty Americans, by virtue of the Volstead Act and the 18th Amendment, could no longer wet themselves down with beer. Since Coca-Cola probably had between two-thirds and three-quarters of the soft drink market at this time, it became the beneficiary of its own size and inertia. Norman Rockwell's paintings of farm boys for Coke are well known; Rockwell's series for Orange Crush are relatively unknown. Hurty Peck Lemon, Hires, Blue Bird — most all of the competitors of Coke — produced fine advertising, but it was overshadowed by the amount of advertising and merchandising done for Coke.

But inexorably tied to America as Coke was, meant, naturally enough, that sales of the drink were affected by the stock market crash and the ensuing depression. Sales peaked at 27.7 million gallons (3.5 billion drinks) in 1930 and then declined — to 26 million gallons (3.3 billion drinks) in 1931, down to 22 million gallons (2.8 billion drinks) the next year, and to 20 million gallons (2.5 billion drinks) in 1933. There was a certain horrific logic to it: a nation out of work wasn't buying cars, radios, refrigerators or apples from the unemployed; and it wasn't buying Coca-Cola either — at least, not in the same quantity as it once had.

Ironically, out of the country's miseries came something The Coca-Cola Company had not faced in many years—an aggressive competitor. The competition, and a healthy success it was too, was Pepsi-Cola.

Pepsi sales had been trickling along after the 1921 bankruptcy. A Wall Street man named Roy Megargel had bought the name, formula, and battered goodwill from the company's creditors, and single-handedly kept the drink in existence by making up its yearly deficits out of his own pocket. Yearly deficits there always were, since Megargel was not a marketing expert; worse still, the only way to make money in the soft drink business is to sell in great volume, and the only way to sell in great volume is to spend a lot of money for advertising and promotion. Megargel didn't have that kind of money himself, and he couldn't raise it.

After the crash, he couldn't afford to make up the deficits, either; and in 1931 Pepsi floated to its second bankruptcy. There the matter might have rested save for a fortuitous circumstance, one of those oddities of American corporate life which has made for a number of millionaires. This particular road to riches is by way of the rebounded insult, wherein a man who feels himself wronged by a corporation promptly goes out and starts his own business in order to revenge himself—if only psychologically—on his former employers. The best example of this in post-war America occurred when the owners of *Esquire* Magazine decided not to give a $5-a-week raise to a guy named Hefner; within 15 years Hefner's *Playboy* was outselling *Esquire* five-to-one, and Hefner was worth a mere $150 million, give or take.

In the matter of Coke and Pepsi, the aggrieved party was a man named Edward Guth, a sharp entrepreneur who had gained control of the Loft's Candy Store chain in 1930. Guth was a tyrannical, mercurial so-and-so, and soon after he consolidated his power in the corporation, he noticed that Loft's was selling a lot of Coke at its soda fountains—an average of over 31,000 gallons a year, or 3.9 million drinks. In Guth's eyes, that volume entitled Loft's to be considered a wholesaler, and be granted the wholesaler's price for Coke syrup. That vision of Loft's place in the world was not shared by the executives of The Coca-Cola Company who in a series of increasingly bitter meetings, turned Guth down.

Finally, Guth sent a memo to one of his vice presidents, wondering about the possibility of doing business with Pepsi-Cola. If impending death does wonders for one's concentration, impending bankruptcy evidently does wonders for one's hearing. Megargel got wind of Guth's interest, and rushed to meet him. The two men hammered out an agreement whereby Megargel would buy the assets of Pepsi-Cola (the trademark, goodwill, and business) at the bankruptcy sale, using money loaned him by Guth. The deal between the two men was fairly complicated, calling for royalty payments to Megargel that Guth didn't make until suit was filed. What remained simple was the continuing failure of Pepsi-Cola to make much of a mark in the soft drink business. Guth, of course, had immediately thrown Coke out of the soda fountains at Loft's, with the immediate result that Loft's soft drink business declined by one-third.

If Pepsi, practically an unknown quantity in New York City, the home base for Loft's, wasn't too good for Loft's fountain business, it was excellent for their legal business. The matter of Coke, Pepsi, and Loft's was to bounce in and out of various courts over the next ten years. The first sticky point lay with the retail transaction. The customer says, "Give me Brand X." Assuming the place serves Brand Y, the fount man or waitress is supposed to tell the customer that he will be getting Brand Y. This works perfectly in theory. In practice, it works for about two days. Either the employee is very busy or tired of taking static from people who demand Brand X and want to know why it isn't served. So he is very likely to serve Brand Y without any explanation. What the hell is he supposed to say to the customer, anyway? Whoever does the serving generally doesn't know why the house serves one brand, rather than another, and so if he is cornered and has to explain, he will generally say that whatever his store serves is exactly the same as whatever it is the customer ordered. "They're all the same, believe me." This is not an endearing statement for soft drink company executives to hear.

What this leads up to, of course, is the fact that The Coca-Cola Company filed suit against Loft's, charging that Pepsi was being substituted for Coke. (Loft's countered with the charge that people representing Coke were patronizing Loft's and loudly defaming Pepsi.) Even if Pepsi were being substituted—and the legal outcome was a draw—it wasn't doing Guth much good. By 1933 Megargel was at his throat for past-due royalties (Guth offered to sell out, Megargel declined, so Guth did the buying out), and Pepsi was doing so poorly that emissaries were sent to Atlanta to find out if The Coca-Cola Company was interested in buying The Pepsi-Cola Company. Atlanta wasn't interested. A year later, it wished it had.

If Pepsi was doing poorly at the fountains, its sales record in bottles was beyond description. Think of the Edsel. Think of Schmeling in the second Louis fight. Think of the San Diego Padres. Pepsi was doing worse than any of these. Things were so rotten that Guth was moved to experimentation. (Moved, perhaps, by the New Deal theory, "Try something. If that doesn't work, try something else. But above all, try *some*thing.") He began to bottle Pepsi in a 12-ounce bottle instead of the "universal" 6-ounce, selling it for a dime. Sales dropped even further; so late in 1933 he tried something else: the 12-ounce bottle for a nickel. Guth had touched the magic button: twice as much as Coke for the same price.

Sales doubled, then doubled again. If the success was immediate, it was still in peril from any other company which might put out a 12-ounce drink for a nickel. Guth moved decisively to ensure that his *coup* would be the base of continued profitability. If the key to profit was volume, then the key to volume was getting Pepsi nationally distributed in a hurry. Guth did for Pepsi what the men from Chattanooga had done for Coke. He picked territorial representatives and gave them the responsibility for enfranchising local bottlers. The inducement was royalties for the reps, royalties which in some cases soared to over $500,000 a year. But if the reps got rich, the company got richer: it showed a profit of over $2 million for 1936, over $3 million for 1937, and over $4 million for 1938.

Although this sudden good fortune on the part of Pepsi must have been painful to the men in Atlanta, still, Coke had rebounded from its sales slump. In part this may have been due to a new invention, the automated fountain mixer, which was introduced at the Chicago World's Fair in 1933. Mixing the exact amount of syrup and carbonated water, it eliminated the possibility of the fount man going light (or heavy) on the syrup.

Where the advertising for Coke in the '30s started out by soliciting testimonials—Joan Crawford was a delicious example (page 115) in view of her later association with Pepsi—it switched to showing various spots around the country (Churchill Downs; an airport in Arizona) where Coke was dispensed. But the advertising was no longer the freewheeling operation, which for example, could put a girl *in front of* the Coke logo (page 44). By 1938 D'Arcy operated with a set of rules for its advertising:

"Following is a list of points which should serve as a guide in preparing any advertising for Coca-Cola. Suggestions will be welcome:

1. Never split the trade mark 'Coca-Cola' in two lines.

2. Any change in the style, color or use of the trade mark must have legal approval.

3. The circular sign should carry the phrase 'Delicious and Refreshing.'

4. The Pause That Refreshes is always to be italicized and avoid splitting it whenever possible.

5. The trade mark must never be obliterated so that it is not perfectly legible unless it is displayed someplace else in the advertisement.

6. The phrase 'trade mark registered' must always appear in the tail of the first 'C' even though it is illegible.

7. Whenever the cooler or bottle or carton or case are shown alone, they should be in color if possible.

8. The phrase 'the six-bottle carton' should appear under the carton when used as a supplementary illustration in magazine advertisements unless specific instructions to the contrary are issued.

9. When a carton is shown, a total of only six bottles should be visible.

10. When the case is shown, a total of not more than twenty-four bottles should be visible.

11. When the cooler is shown open, the righthand side which shows the bottle opener should be opened if possible.

12. Until further notice, always use the bottle which says 'Bottle Pat. D-105529' and check each time to find out which side of the bottle to show.

13. Use as few different type faces and sizes as possible on any advertisement.

14. Never use a picture of a crowd of people taken as a 'candid shot' because releases are not available.

15. Always secure legal releases from all persons or names of persons shown in an advertisement.

16. Copyright and signature 'The Coca-Cola Company' to appear on all magazine, trade paper and newspaper advertisements run by the company—not in bottler advertisements or on posters.

17. On oil paintings or color photographs be inclined to show a brunette rather than a blonde girl if only one girl is in the picture. Otherwise, show both.

18. In any illustration remember—adolescent girls or young women should be the wholesome type; not sophisticated-looking. Boys or young men should be wholesome, healthy types; not too handsome or sophisticated. Seldom show very old people, and never children under 6 or 7 years old.

19. Clothing, including hats, should be modern and up-to-date, but not extreme.

20. The Coca-Cola 'red, green and yellow' must be rigidly followed in color work.

21. The color of the full bottle should be standardized and reproduced in accordance with most recent instructions or information. [A color photograph of Coca-Cola looks like a color photograph of mud, or carbonated mud. Photographers doing work for the Company have always had a devilish time trying to make the drink look like the drink.]

22. All original copy must have legal approval.

23. Never use the trade mark in a descriptive sense or in any sense except as the name of the drink.

24. Never refer to Coca-Cola as 'it.'

25. Always say '<u>the pause that refreshes</u> with ice-cold Coca-Cola' — never use it as synonymous with Coca-Cola.

26. Never use Coca-Cola in a personal sense — such as, 'Coca-Cola invites you to lunch.'

27. Never make any exaggerated claim in copy beyond the fact that it [see rule #24] is a 'delicious, refreshing, wholesome, pure drink — easily available.'

28. Never show or imply that Coca-Cola should be drink [sic] by very young children.

29. Whenever the company's name is used, say 'The Coca-Cola Company.'

30. Never use a song, music, words, or title without a release.

31. Never use a phrase or slogan without first checking our rights to use it, if any.

32. Never infer that Coca-Cola should be bought by phone.

33. When asking people to buy, be sure it is perfectly clear that you mean 'from your dealer,' and not from the bottler or the company.

34. Proof from the first plates completed for any magazine advertisement should be submitted to Atlanta for approval whenever time permits.

35. Approval on sample posters should be obtained from Atlanta before releasing from lithographer."

If such rigidity in the creation of advertising is symptomatic of big business, then the Company was justified. Coca-Cola was indisputably big business. By the late '30s, over $5.5 million a year was being spent for advertising in all its forms.

In much the same way that a big American sedan does certain things well (and certain things horribly), D'Arcy was brilliant in some areas, and obviously, aaahhh, *strange* in others. One of those others was radio. In 1933 a D'Arcy employee named Gilson Gray began to investigate the ways in which the agency could use radio for advertising Coke. Two of his memos give evidence of the sometimes peculiar goings-on at D'Arcy.

May 2nd, 1933

Mr. Lee:

As a starting point, I think we must recognize the fact that radio, at least from the point of view of the great mass of listeners, is purely a medium of entertainment. They turn to it to be diverted, to be amused, to be taken outside themselves. The advertiser is able to capitalize on this desire for diversion to the extent and in the proportion that his particular program does arouse the interest of the mass of listeners. His advertising message as such has nothing to do with this interest. The listeners' attitude is, strictly speaking, one which puts up with the advertising in order to get the entertainment. We must then also recognize the fact that advertising is a forced growth on radio.

For this reason radio can never be as direct an advertising medium as other forms of media. It must have its greatest force as a medium of good will. And it has, therefore, always seemed to me that it is best suited as a medium to products that are so well known that mere mention almost amounts to description and to products whose selling points do not require a detailed specification of mechanical features.

However, Coca-Cola happens to be a product which is peculiarly adapted to whatever promotional force radio can offer. And if, for whatever reasons, Coca-Cola desires to do something spectacular, radio naturally suggests itself because it is undoubtedly the most conspicuous addition which could be made to Coca-Cola's present activities . . .

It has become increasingly apparent that the most successful programs of entertainment are those which bring to the air the same elements of showmanship which have proved most successful in the theatre. Yet while the elements are the same, there are distinct differences in technique. However, these are recognized and the best production brains of the show business are constantly studying them and are increasingly eager to put their ideas into form. There are tremendous possibilities in this direction in the creation of new and novel forms of entertainment.

On the program side of the experiment I would engage the outstanding production and direction brains of the show business to produce a series of complete, original plays with music, each to be especially written for the air. By this I mean that each week's show would be produced and directed by a different well-known leader of the show business. Under his supervision a complete original manuscript would be prepared, music, lyrics and comedy all specially written for this show just as it would be for an original Broadway production. Leading writers, outstanding composers, like Jerome Kern, George Gershwin, Cole Porter, Sigmund Romberg, etc., would be engaged for each show and the casts would be the finest that could be assembled. Obviously, a different group would do each week's show and each group would be endeavoring for its effort to produce the finest original radio entertainment yet devised. Each program would necessarily have to be at least an hour in length in order to accommodate the scope of a complete musical play each performance.

On the advertising side, I would make a radical experiment. In the belief that radio cannot be made a truly direct advertising medium, I would not make the slightest attempt to force it to be such. I would make absolutely certain that no listener could mistake the fact that these spectacular radio shows were presented by Coca-Cola; because they would be so different both in entertainment and in the presentation of advertising, I would tie them to Coca-Cola as the pause that refreshes on the air, and tie Coca-Cola to it all as the drink that makes a pause refreshing. But beyond that, in the accepted idea of commercial announcements on the air, I would not go, except for the references to be outlined below.

Because newspapers are essentially a highly direct advertising medium, I would turn to them for the full force of direct, reason-why, bounce-back-to-normal, smash advertising. Each afternoon of the night the radio program would be broadcast, I would run one of these advertisements in the evening paper in each city in which the program would be broadcast. These would be straightforward Coca-Cola advertisements except that, in addition, they would in prominent type invite the reader to listen to the spectacular experiment in pure entertainment to be broadcast that evening.

At least at the outset of the radio series, I would announce on the air briefly but quite frankly just what was being done and what kind of experiment was being made both as to program and as to advertising procedure. I would announce to the listeners that they and they alone would judge this spectacular experiment; that we would judge their verdict by what they said and by sales results, and that while we earnestly requested their writing us what they thought of the experiment, we would offer no give-away for their letters since we did not desire to influence them to write for any other reason than their honest reaction. At the end of the program and perhaps also at the beginning we would, instead of the usual commercial, refer them to the advertisement in the evening paper.

I am convinced that this combination use of radio and newspapers would not only make the most spectacular effort Coca-Cola could possibly engage in, but also would concentrate on Coca-Cola a promotional force such as has not before been experienced—a completely well-rounded force, in that each medium would be used for what each can best accomplish, each supplying exactly what the other lacks.

Just in advance of the start of the campaign and along with the orders to the advertising managers of the newspapers in question, I would send a complete story stating exactly what the campaign and experiment was all about and how we felt that the newspapers supplied a force we couldn't do without in the complete effort. In view of the newspaper-radio controversy, it is my belief that every paper in question will play up the story rather big, possibly in the news columns and at least in the radio columns.

In addition there is another newspaper angle. Should a spectacular radio program alone be presented, it would certainly not make any newspaper friends for Coca-Cola and in view of the present situation regarding taxes, beer and liquor, newspaper friends would be extremely valuable. So from a policy viewpoint as well as a promotion viewpoint, the use of newspapers would add tremendous force and in addition publicize to a highly valuable extent the experiment as a whole.

I have constantly referred to this program as an experiment. I think it should constantly be looked upon and presented as that. I think it draws added strength as such. The network would want it to succeed. The newspapers would want it to succeed, for here truly would be a radio campaign which actually brought them real business. And the public would want it to succeed, if as I feel it would, it brought them what they wanted in a way that would please them and still work on them powerfully.

While the experiment would entail a very large outlay in appropriation, I feel sure that at the end of thirteen weeks we would know absolutely if it were worthwhile. If it proved so, it could be continued. If it did not prove so, it could be cancelled at the end of what after all is a comparatively short time, and at a very minimum we would have accomplished, I believe, the original intent, which is to do the most spectacular thing possible for a time for policy reasons . . .

Gilson Gray
July 31, 1933

If you can believe it, the first two paragraphs of Gray's memo actually represented the perceived relationship between advertising and the broadcast media in the early days of advertising on radio. The relationship in that form, obviously, did not last long.

Gray's fantasy programming was a bit more than the traffic would bear. Within a few months, though, he had a new plan:

Mr. Lee:

This will serve as a resumé of our Coca-Cola radio activities at the moment and also as a registration of my firm personal conviction that we have in our hands the makings of the outstanding radio program of the year.

I discussed the thought of completely original musical comedies, each to be produced by one of the outstanding producers of New York and each to be written and composed by the outstanding men in their line, as outlined to you in my memorandum on the subject early in May. And everyone with whom I discussed it, including John Royal and Frank Black at NBC as well as Gus Haenschen, all jumped at it as the absolute ultimate in radio—the finest thing that could ever be done.

But granting that, it is also full of difficulties. The organization of it would be a man-killing job. All the necessary elements, the composers, etc., are notoriously hard to handle, as are the producers, and you would never be sure of getting material on time or have any guarantee that it would be right when you got it. All of them, including the producers, in line with show business practice would demand advances of no inconsiderable sum before going to work. In fact one or two big producers who were approached before I left New York immediately started talking about $5,000 on the line in advance. Finally the whole thing would be horribly expensive and probably beyond our reach. However, as long as we have started on the idea, we are carrying through and will know in a short time whether or not the idea is practical to do at all, what the conditions would be and approximately how much it would cost.

While we were canvassing this whole thought we came upon another idea that seems ideal in every respect, with all the tremendous publicity value of the other but at the same time intensely practical from a production standpoint and made up of proved material that we know all about in advance.

We can get the rights to all the outstanding operettas of Europe by the leading composers, all of which have been produced abroad successfully and not one of which has ever been done either on the air or on the stage in this country. Frank Black already has twenty-six of them in his office and there are many more of them available— all we would ever need—and more being produced all the time. They are by such outstanding men as Lehar who wrote "The Merry Widow," Strauss whom everyone knows, Robert Stoltz who wrote "Two Hearts in Waltz Time" and others.

Frank Black played me music from many of them and it is extremely refreshing. No one here is writing such melody. We go in too much for rhythm music. It is all fresh and new and the operettas are delightful with romance, comedy and real plot interest.

It is such a thing as has never been done on the air. It is particularly fitting to Coca-Cola for all the music is fresh and new and it has enormous publicity value. We could of course cast it superbly with a different group of stars each week and we all want to start it off with Jeritza in the leading role of the first one, because she not only is marvelous but is Viennese herself. In addition, we could easily arrange with the publishers, I'm sure, to have the hit song of each operetta printed for distribution to be given away as we see fit, either free or for bottle caps or whatever scheme we might devise.

To my mind this idea has everything the first thought had with none of the difficulties and none of the gambles. Every program would be a first night on the air with all the delightful freshness that so fits Coca-Cola. Frank Black and NBC are now putting one of these in complete shape for the air and for audition and we'll have all details in about two weeks or maybe a little more. It would naturally have to be an hour show. It just couldn't be done in less.

Frankly, I feel happier about having something real for Coca-Cola than I have in a long time. I think we have the opportunity to grab the air, so to speak, with a marvelous program that can't help but get all the publicity in the world plus the fact that it would be a superb show and a really beautiful vehicle for the Coca-Cola story.

Gilson Gray

However much Gray's thinking of July represented a dimming of his creative flame (as might be said in a 1933 novel about advertising agencies), it was still no small potatoes for a medium which considered hot stuff to be Jacques Renard playing a fiddle in a small studio. Gray was still operating on a level which today would be called 440 cubes, factory air, power steering, power seats, power windows, power power, and sixteen-track tape deck.

The other way of going at it—achieving product recognition through radio—was used for Pepsi. In 1939, a year in which advertising expenditures for Coke were over $6,100,000, Alan Bradley Kent and Austen Herbert Croom were paid the grand sum of $2500 for writing a new set of lyrics to go with the melody of an old

English hunting song, *D'ye Ken John Peel*. A year later *Life* Magazine called the words "immortal":

> Pepsi-Cola hits the spot
> Twelve full ounces, that's a lot
> Twice as much for a nickel, too
> Pepsi-Cola is the drink for you.

At the turn of the decade, a momentous court case, Coke vs. Pepsi in the area of trademark infringement, was making its way through the courts. Coke was to lose that battle, but it was about to win a war.

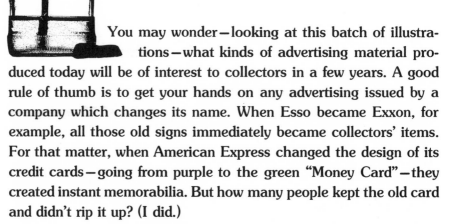

CHAPTER 12

You may wonder—looking at this batch of illustrations—what kinds of advertising material produced today will be of interest to collectors in a few years. A good rule of thumb is to get your hands on any advertising issued by a company which changes its name. When Esso became Exxon, for example, all those old signs immediately became collectors' items. For that matter, when American Express changed the design of its credit cards—going from purple to the green "Money Card"—they created instant memorabilia. But how many people kept the old card and didn't rip it up? (I did.)

The only danger in collecting this kind of material—aside from the clutter it will cause in your home—is that it may produce a temperament unsuitable to performing certain jobs, like speculating in real estate (which means ripping down old buildings). This may be the best argument yet for being a collector.

These two trays were used for carrying change to drugstore customers. The Coke tray dates from 1905. The Moxie tray is c. 1920.

The tray at top is the earliest known example of a Coke tray, dating from 1898. The one at bottom was put out by those devils in Chicago c.1907. Both trays are incredibly rare and valuable to collectors, with the 1898 tray selling for a mere $1000. The nude is cheap at $500-750.

This change
tray, from
1904 com-
memorated the
St. Louis Expo-
sition of that
year.

This serving tray is the oldest known piece of metal advertising for Pepsi. The paper label on the Pepsi bottle was obviously copied from the paper label used on Coke bottles of the period. In celebration of the Company's 75th anniversary, copies of this tray have been issued in 1973.

The top serving tray dates from c. 1910. If one assumes that the fellow shown is a doctor, one can only think that he was the father of Dr. Sivana. The bottom tray, painted by Harry Morse Meyers, dates from 1915.

The "Betty"
tray, issued
in 1914.

"Hilda Clark" was produced in 1904.

This 1905 tray marked one of the last quasi-medicinal claims for Coke.

A 1930 tray.

A Nu-Grape
tray c. 1928.
The Pepsi
tray was put
out in the early
'30s, and tried
to make the
point that Pepsi
was no regional
drink.

The tray at top
is from 1927.
Johnny
Weissmuller
and Maureen
O'Sullivan
are on the
1934 tray.

Another 1930 tray.

Hayden Hayden
painted this
1932 tray.

The Nehi tray dates from the mid-'30s.

You might think that this 1936 tray, known by collectors as "Society Girl," was posed by Myrna Loy. If you did, you'd be wrong. It was Lillian Bond.

CHAPTER 13

If there was any irony in the battle between Coke and Pepsi (and it is hard to work up suitable irony when battalions—regiments—of high-priced lawyers are having at each other) it was that Charles Guth, the man who had made a success of Pepsi, was forced out of control of the drink. He had used Loft money to finance the purchase of Pepsi; he had used Loft personnel to market the drink. In short, he had been playing a version of the old shell game, Guess Where Guth's Money Is, and he was finally ambushed by dissident Loft stockholders who saw their corporation falling apart as its chief executive officer devoted most of his time to a soft drink. After Guth was jettisoned and Loft's real control of Pepsi-Cola was established, the new management found that Pepsi was indeed á more valuable piece of goods than bon bons; they sold off the candy stores and reincorporated as The Pepsi-Cola Company.

A nagging question remained, however; how much of a soft drink would they have left to merchandise if they were denied the use of the name Pepsi-Cola? It is easy, at least in retrospect, to understand the very human basis of the infringement suit. Stung by the sudden sales effervescence of Pepsi, horrified and deeply angered by the substitution of Pepsi for Coke in Loft's stores, The Coca-Cola Company had retaliated by filing suit—in Canada, where the Pepsi name was new. Years later, *Fortune* magazine was to speculate that the suit never would have been brought had Harold Hirsch stayed with the Company. But Hirsch, the demon legal expert, had clashed repeatedly with Robert Woodruff, both of them being strong-willed men, and had resigned from the Company, not before, however, advising against the Pepsi suit. Hirsch evidently didn't think that the courts would sustain the position advanced by The Coca-Cola Company of Canada, Ltd., and he probably also knew that the implications of a lost suit might go far beyond competition from Pepsi. In the past, the success of the legal department of The Coca-Cola Company in winning trademark cases had the effect of keeping many firms from marketing cola drinks with the word "cola" in the brand name. Tolerating the existence of Pepsi would do little to alter that situation. Losing the suit, however, would open the gates for a host of cola drinks with "cola" as part of their names—drinks which otherwise might have been marketed under any number of dissimilar names. Remember Quencher.

To make the whole affair a little more preposterous, the plaintiff (The Coca-Cola Company of Canada, Ltd.) did not introduce evidence showing confusion between the two trademarks. but offered only a *likelihood* of confusion based—brace yourself—on the similarities in the script used in the respective trade marks.

The Exchequer Court of Canada, the trial court, held for the position of Coca-Cola, three cheers from Atlanta. Then the Supreme Court of Canada reversed the decision, saying that the marks themselves were not *that* similar, and besides, there had been no evidence that anyone had been misled (in Canada, anyway). In 1942, the inevitable appeal reached The Privy Council—the highest judicial body in the United Kingdom, and one which had final decision over all matters tried in Commonwealth courts. The Privy Council upheld the Canadian Supreme Court, ruling that since no errors had been committed in the reversal, it would stand. There was no joy in Georgia that day, and since second-guessing judicial decisions is a hobby almost as popular as second-guessing football quarterbacks, it comes as no shock that there are, even today, a few executives of The Coca-Cola Company who will quietly speculate that The Privy Council was not—at the darkest moment in the war—about to reverse the highest court of a Commonwealth ally.

Although the decision didn't result in any rush of strong new competition—Royal Crown Cola is the only brand which comes to mind as being introduced in that period and since it was marketed in a 12-ounce bottle, it was more competition for Pepsi than Coke—the court case did contribute to some marvelous mythology about Coke. While the "cola litigation" (as it is known in the legal department of The Coca-Cola Company) was plodding through the courts, the Atlanta lawyers noted that, whatever the outcome of the litigation, the entire compound-hyphenated word "Coca-Cola" was registered. But the position of the registration notice (good old Regus Patoff) was in the tail of the "C" of "Coca-," which made it appear to the unsophisticated that only "Coca-" was registered. Move the notice, said the lawyers, to a point under the hyphen, straddling the "Coca-" and the "-Cola." That decision necessitated redrawing the trademark script (chubbier before the war), and gave rise, once the registration notice was moved, to the terrific nonsense that the court had ruled for Pepsi *because* the notice for Coca-Cola had been put in the tail of the "C" and therefore didn't protect the entire name. This marvelous canard, which absolutely stinks of plausibility, has been printed in newspapers and magazines up to the present, and has, once and for all, no basis in fact.

While Coke and Pepsi were metaphorically hitting each other over the head with rolled up depositions, real competition was being ignored. A St. Louis businessman named Charles L. Grigg had gone into the soft drink business in 1920, after being fired from a position with a bottler who was tired of Grigg's frequent observations about the correct way to run the business. Grigg and a coal merchant named Edmund Ridgway started bottling an orange drink named "Howdy," which enjoyed a fair success until citrus growers, unable to move as much of their goods as they wished, rammed through legislation in several states requiring orange-flavored drinks to contain real orange pulp and orange juice. Grigg immediately began experimenting with other flavors, finally settling on a lemon-lime mixture. There were, at the time, only 600-odd lemon-lime soft drinks on the market, but Grigg began bottling and distributing his, calling it 7-Up. The Seven part of the name is obvious, the drink being bottled in seven-ounce containers, but the origin of the Up probably had something to do with the fact that the drink used to be unusually powerful in the carbonation department. Grigg had first introduced 7-Up in October, 1929, just in time for the stock market crash. Considering what he felt was the drink's obvious asset, the timing was strangely fortuitous.

An advertising booklet put out by the company in the late '30s explained its many uses in 14 pages of vignettes. Under a cartoon of a man smiling with a stogie in his mouth, a headline ran "Pa Gets An Idea." The text went:

> Reading a scientific article on "Why Spas Benefit" Pa discovered that in drinking the water charged with gas or CO_2 the charged water should not be agitated nor stirred to waste the gas. He found the gas was the thing. So Pa began to drink 7-Up. First for the big charge of gas—then for the effect of 7-Up in the stomach.

That was okay for starters; the rest of the booklet was truly inspired:

> Ma's Metabolism. Ma got to talking about her metabolism a while back and Pa finally told her to forget it or go to a doctor and at least find out what the word meant. Pa told her that as long as she kept on eating like a bird at noon when he wasn't home, she was bound to feel listless in the afternoon. So now she drinks a bottle of 7-Up around 3 o'clock, and it peps her up. She watched the scales for awhile, but found 7-Up didn't add any weight and now she's happy.
>
> "Riled Up" from Riding. A lady taking a two-day auto ride became "all riled up" as she put it and stopped for a rest. Someone told her to drink a bottle of 7-Up. She did—and 7-Up did. Her stomach came back in a few minutes. She took some 7-Up along and prevented all such "riling." If a short ride, drink 7-Up before starting. If a long one, take some along.
>
> Entertainment Simplified. Your guests are not hungry when they come to you but refreshments are quite necessary to complete the occasion. 7-Up served at parties adds to the zest of things. On the first appearance of lassitude serve 7-Up in pretty glasses and hear the praises of every guest. Every one likes 7-Up, no matter whether old or young. 7-Up is the ideal Fresh Up party drink. One lady upset a glass of 7-Up on her dainty luncheon cloth. She was greatly perturbed, expecting stain but to her surprise there was no stain.
>
> Winter Foods. Richer than in the summer with less exercise to

help burn it properly and drinking less water, often bring on our winter troubles. Drink 7-Up freely. Being highly carbonated 7-Up tends to activate the stomach and is an aid in relieving the distressed feeling after heavy meals. In the evening, along about yawning time, open a cool bottle and "Fresh Up" with 7-Up. Keep a case in the house and enjoy it more and more. Drink 7-Up Cool, not too cold—40° or lower suppresses the flavor in anything.

Mental Lassitude. Mental Lassitude resulting from a heavy meal or certain forms of indigestion occasionally gets the student or reader. Your mind seems far away, you can't concentrate. At this point "Fresh up" with 7-Up and help clear away those cobwebs. Get a cool bottle, relax and enjoy its goodness. Then back to your work with renewed pep. Food is not a Medicine. 7-Up is not a Medicine. Both are good for you.

Slenderizing? To reduce weight you must reduce food. A reducing diet punishes—you have a craving. Then you should drink a small bottle of 7-Up. It satisfies this craving. It is a quick burner and adds nothing to adipose tissue. Using 7-Up this way contributes no little to the slenderizing effect and helps avoid punishment common to reducing diets. And, remember, 7-Up is a friendly "Fresh up" drink. Drink 7-Up cool—not cold—and never stir out the gas.

What Is 7-Up? A water-white visibly pure drink bottled for purity's sake. A softly acid drink that does not irritate. Lemon and Limes are used to flavor and make palatable and these two flavors are the best possible boosters for other flavors used as a mixer. They bring up the finest bouquet. The heavy charge of CO_2 or gas, sets 7-Up aside from the usual. Do not stir or agitate 7-Up before drinking, pour gently and get the gas inside you where it can do some good. To waste in the air is all wrong. You owe it to yourself to get 7-Up because of its great difference. Bouquet comes up best at 60° to 70°. 7-Up brings up flavor.

At Your Best. To go to your work with head up, chest out, ready for the business of the day is really worthwhile. The use of 7-Up on retiring or even on arising aids in restoring normal conditions, and as a result 7-Up is held in high regard by both men and women. Keep 7-Up in your refrigerator. Chill it. Don't use ice. It drinks best at just a cool temperature and does the most good. 7-Up is very inexpensive. You can get it in 5¢ bottles or larger bottles.

Now Grandma Laughs. Grandma was old—Grandma was unable to retain anything in her stomach. Her son drove a long way to see her and having some 7-Up in his car proceeded to give some to Grandma. It stayed down. They gave her more and more. She lived on 7-Up for three days. She began to eat again—now after two years she laughs and drinks 7-Up regularly. 7-Up in bottles only—for purity's sake.

Nurse says—7-Up Stays Down When Water Won't. In the sick room 7-Up is a great help by its action in the stomach. In some cases where necessary foods or liquids won't stay down, 7-Up will as it is less irritating. Fever patients like 7-Up because of its pleasant taste and it quenches their thirst better than water, just as it quenches your thirst on a hot day. The food properties of 7-Up are quickly absorbed and 7-Up is appreciated by all who use it in the sick room, because of its pleasant taste. Every bottle is sterilized.

What Does Hang-Over Mean to You? To most people the word hang-over is essentially the alcoholic 'morning after.' Some people over eat, others over worry, others over work. Various excesses bring punishment. Over smoking produces a woozy feeling, call it a hang-over or what you like. A cold bottle of 7-Up tastes mighty good. You like it—it likes you and is a wonderful aid in restoring normal conditions. Chill in your refrigerator. Drink cool, omit ice.

"Don't Stir 7-Up. It mixes without stirring. Pour 7-Up gently on the side of the glass—See it mix . . . To stir releases the gas—the carbon dioxide—you so need in the system. When you take the "cure" at the Spas it is the carbon dioxide that benefits so much and the drinking of the charged water. There is much more CO_2 in a bottle of 7-Up than in several glasses of natural CO_2 water. Most people stir, shake or fizz 7-Up and waste this 'life gas.' Such drinks are flat—lifeless. When you use seltzer from a siphon it looks fine as it fizzes, but when you drink it the CO_2 is gone. It is flat. So take a tip pour 7-Up gently on the side of the glass, and remember 7-Up need not be very cold—just cool. Avoid ice in the glass. Don't stir, shake or fizz.

And, finally for those who found life-giving properties in other beverages:

> 7-Up Brings Up the Flavor of All Liquor and Wine. When alcohol was in general use the heavy sour acid sodas were used to cover the taste. With flavory liquors a softly acid soda like 7-Up is used to intensify the bouquet. A revelation awaits you when you use 7-Up as a mixer. Do not stir or fizz. Pour gently. If 7-Up is cool, you need no ice. Cold suppresses bouquet. 7-Up from the cooler is just right.

It would take twenty years for 7-Up to worry the makers of Coke and Pepsi. In the meantime, the St. Louis owners would have to discover for themselves what Asa Candler had hit on — that medicinal drinks are limited in their appeal. To make 7-Up more *generally* refreshing, that big blast of "life gas" was reduced to more manageable proportions (leading Grace Sultan of Chicago, a connoisseur in this area, to note bitterly that "they took the *grepps* [belch] out of the *greppswasser*").

For the duration of the war, the combat in soft drinks was between Coke and Pepsi. And Pepsi hardly had time to revel in the favorable court decision before being declared wartime casualty in the marketplace. Domestically, workers in war plants had enough money not to have to buy twice as much for a nickle unless they wanted to. Furthermore, sugar rationing slowed any further surge in Pepsi sales. If all that weren't bad enough, Coke was to Pepsi overseas as Patton was to the Wehrmacht.

A month after Pearl Harbor, Harrison Jones, soon to be named board chairman of The Coca-Cola Company, grimly told his associates to prepare for rationing. The first thing the Company did was to lay in a huge stock of sugar, a snappy ploy also tried by The Pepsi-Cola Company. The government just as promptly bought back most of this supply from both firms. Atlanta executives then applied to Washington for the right to control rationing from Atlanta, an easier system for everyone concerned than trying to ration through the thousand-odd bottlers. Company executives were dispatched to ransack the corporate files to find out what had been done regarding rationing during World War I. Those records, however, had been destroyed or lost (a mistake not repeated; the World War II rationing files were dusted off for use during the Korean War, and today sit in the company archives, waiting on an emergency).

In February, 1942, the government announced a "base year" against which rationing could be measured. The year 1941 was selected, and for the remainder of the war, soft drink companies each month had a quota of from 50 percent to 80 percent of the production they had attained in the same month of the base year. The only exception from base year regulations—and what a nice exception it was, too—was for sales to the armed forces. Bottlers in such cities as San Diego and Charleston, Lawton, Oklahoma, and Watertown, N.Y., suddenly found themselves with a swollen military market and the absolute right to purvey as much soda pop as the military wanted to soak up. Of course, bottlers in other locations, ones without *giant* military installations nearby, found themselves suffering, unable to meet the civilian demand, forced indeed, to discourage it.

These bottlers found themselves with a lot of unused production capacity. The Coca-Cola Company took care of that. Robert Woodruff had vowed that any serviceman, at home *or overseas,* who wanted a Coke would be able to get one for 5¢. Behind the deep, genuine patriotism in that promise was a neat bit of calculation. The only way to get Coca-Cola to the troops—given the fact that transports couldn't be used to carry hundreds of millions of Coke bottles back and forth—was to build bottling plants where the troops were. Looking ahead to the day when the war was won, though the troops would come home, there was no reason why the bottling plants had to. Those plants would make Coca-Cola, once and for all, in one giant sweep, a truly global drink. The only difficulty lay in finding bottling equipment to send overseas. No such machinery was being manufactured, so the obvious solution was for the Company to buy from its bottlers any underutilized bottling equipment. Human nature being what it was and is, some of those bottlers were loath to part with their machines: *what if* an army base were put up outside town? The Company found a novel way of sweetening the deal . . . literally. In the course of making the syrup in Atlanta, there is, normally, some sugar spilled. What is normal spillage in peacetime is, in war, an amount which can be swept up, cleaned, and used to make an amount of syrup in excess of quota allotments, that syrup to be distributed to those poor devils who served only civilian markets, and whose machines were being carted off to war.

The machines that were being carted off were assembled into the second-greatest invasion force of the war. This metaphor isn't as anthropomorphic as it might at first seem—a Disney cartoon of hundreds of smiling (yet somehow stern) machines walking, in a funny side-to-side rocking gait, through Europe and across the Pacific—since the Company conducted its own human mobilization, putting a couple of hundred employees in uniform. They were known as TOs, technical observers, who wore officer's uniforms without insignia, and who were afforded the perquisites of a commissioned officer. In fact, it can be assumed that they were afforded the perquisites of high-ranking officers, since it was their technical skills which kept the Coke coming. (The TOs suffered dangers, some half-dozen of them being killed in the course of the war.)

They adapted the equipment to fit in Jeeps for use in the jungle, followed the troops into Paris and instantly rebuilt the bottling plant there (helped in this by the fact that Eisenhower was a long-time Coke freak, his love of the drink speeding equipment requisitions). In Egypt, they hired Arabs to man the bottling equipment, teaching them Western standards of hygiene, a process that was considerably shortened when the Arabs found that the mandatory showers didn't necessarily have to be hot. Which made for a new problem—dragging the men out of the *cool* showers.

There are thousands of anecdotes about the role that Coke played in the war—from the bomb runs made over Japanese airstrips using empty Coke bottles as projectiles (Coke runs, they were called); to the auctioning off for charity of a single bottle of Coke for $4000; to planes sent from the combat zone, thousands of miles away, to Australia, where they would fill up with Coke; to Ike specifically ordering that ten bottling plants follow his troops into North Africa.

While all of this was going on, you might assume that the only sound heard in the offices of The Pepsi-Cola Company near the East River in New York would have been the sound of gnashing teeth. Aahh, but there was also a mean chortle or two. If volume was the key to profitability, and if rationing cut volume, then the trick was to increase that volume. Any idiot could see that. The only way to increase volume, however, was to get more sugar, and that was impossible. Mexico, for example, had a lot of sugar, but if sugar was brought into the United States from Mexico, it would fall under the rules of rationing, and be taken away by the government. The solution for The Pepsi-Cola Company was to build a plant just over the border in Mexico, where sugar would be processed into something that wasn't *quite* syrup. This stuff—it was called "El Masco," but it should have been called El Sneako—was brought into the country and distributed to bottlers, quite legally, until 1944, when the government finally decided that it was *so* sugar, and halted importation.

All this while, the advertising of Coca-Cola was celebrating its success in the war effort. Where other industries could and did show their products being used in gory combat, Coke obviously wasn't being used on the enemy. Instead, a series of magazine ads were produced explaining how slogans pertaining to Coke were translated in other languages—the languages of allies in the war. The paintings showed American troops drinking Coke with their counterparts in other armed forces, or with liberated civilians. For example, a 1943 ad had a painting of American flyers and Chinese troops holding bottles of Coke in front of a bullet-spattered P-40 (the nose of the plane painted with the dragon motif made famous by the Flying Tigers). The copy proclaimed, "Have a 'Coke'—Good winds have blown you here. A way to say 'We are friends' to the Chinese." Obviously, there was a lot of poetic license used in the ads.

The first thing that leaps out from the ad is the fact that Coke was finally Coke. While the Pepsi case was dragging on, The Coca-Cola Company finally decided to do formally what increasing numbers of customers were doing informally—calling its product Coke. It started using the word in 1941, building up a library of usage so that, by 1945, Coke could join Coca-Cola as registered trademarks of the Company. In places like this 1943 ad, the use of "Coke" was explained in a separate text block: "'Coke' = Coca-Cola. It's natural for popular names to acquire friendly abbreviations. That's why you hear Coca-Cola called 'Coke'".

The rest of the ad addressed itself, however obliquely, to the war: "In far-off places, when Coca-Cola is on hand, you find it cementing friendships for our fighting men. China knew Coca-Cola from Tientsin to Shanghai, from Hong Kong to Tsingtao. To Chinese and Yank alike, *Have a 'Coke'* are welcome words. They belong with friendliness and freedom. From Atlanta to the Seven Seas, Coca-Cola stands for *the pause that refreshes*—has become a symbol of good will among the friendly-minded." Almost as an after-thought, another text block hinted at how the Coke was getting into that picture: "Our fighting men are delighted to meet up with Coca-Cola many places overseas. Coca-Cola has been a globe-trotter 'since way back when.' Even with war, Coca-Cola today is being bottled on the spot in over 35 allied and neutral nations."

It was during the war that D'Arcy finally came to grips with radio. Starting in December, 1941, the weekly "Spotlight Bands" program was not only spectacular (for the period), but remarkably effective in promoting goodwill for Coke. The remote broadcasts from industrial plants and armed forces installations not only were good for the war effort, but also featured the best in big bands, from Artie Shaw and Harry James to Count Basie and Duke Ellington.

There was no tin for new signs to put at new retail outlets, or to replace older ones that might be rusted. There was no way to expand the market, since there was no way to satisfy the demand of the rationed society. All that could be done for Coke was to keep the name in front of the public, electronically, with the softest of all soft sells. "Spotlight Bands" was judged to be perfect for that job.

As the war ended, one might have thought that Robert Woodruff would have studied enough of the life of Woodrow Wilson to know that it indeed isn't enough to win a war if you don't win the peace that follows.

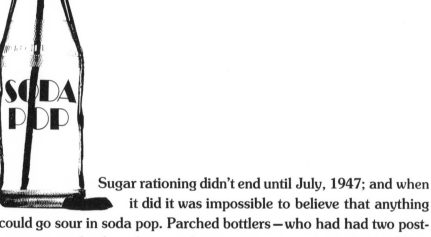

CHAPTER 14

Sugar rationing didn't end until July, 1947; and when it did it was impossible to believe that anything could go sour in soda pop. Parched bottlers—who had had two postwar years to beef up their production capacity—responded by filling more bottles than ever before. The Atlanta bottler of Coca-Cola, working round the clock in the sultry days of late summer, actually managed to turn out 1,000,000 bottles of Coke in 48 hours. It was a sales boom of epic proportions (1948 was the best year yet for Coca-Cola, with gross sales of nearly $235 million; in 1949 the net profits after taxes were almost $38 million, an interesting figure when you think that gross *sales* in 1929 had been $39 million).

Two things, however, were working against the Company. The first was an industry-wide phenomenon: inflation. Unlike the wage-price spiral of the early '20s, which had cooled out with 5¢ still worth something (a bottle of Coke, anyway), the post-World War II inflation started squeezing the bottlers in 1946 and kept on through the Korean War. The obvious solution was to raise prices, but bottlers found that raising their prices meant a loss of volume. And the loss in volume meant lower revenues. Looking back at the first giddy rush of postwar sales, one executive of The Coca-Cola Company recalls sadly, "We were filling the pipes that had been dry for so long, but we sure weren't expanding into new markets."

The new market was going to be discovered by Alfred Steele, a vice president of The Coca-Cola Company, who committed the unpardonable sin of leaving the mother church to work for the devil—that is, in 1949 he went to work for The Pepsi-Cola Company, taking some 15 key men with him, including a bunch from the market research department. It probably was a case of perfectly matched desperations: Steele looked at the hierarchy in Atlanta and determined that he wasn't going to go far enough, fast enough; at Pepsi headquarters, the inflation was producing business reverses of a sort that guarantee quick promotion for the man who could stem them.

With Pepsi producing one-quarter the volume and one-quarter the revenue of Coke, it is clear that any wiggling to counter the inflation spiral hurt the Pepsi-Cola Company more. As profits declined, budgets were cut, which meant less promotion and advertising, which meant . . . well, you get the drift. Ironically, one of Steele's apparently mechanical problems was in exactly the area which was going to provide the company's greatest growth. Both major soft drink manufacturers were being crippled by the fact that their biggest bottlers, the ones in the largest cities, were being severely hurt by distribution problems in the cities. The plants were capable of turning out enough product, but there was no way to get the product to the retail outlet efficiently. More trucks and drivers had been added to service the greater number of outlets and to try and overwhelm the traffic jams through sheer numbers. Well, that latter tactic didn't work, and since the loading facilities at the plants hadn't been constructed for so many trucks, lines of empty trucks would stand outside the plants, waiting to get in. Obviously, the answer was decentralization of facilities.

That was a good enough technical answer for the bottlers, but what it indicated to Steele and his market research guys was that the America of the old ads for Coca-Cola was changing. The constituency of those ads—small-town America on the one hand, a super-urbanity on the other—had been torn apart. It was the beginnings of the upward-striving middle class, an urban middle class, whose style—all those young vets—was different than before. Since Steele didn't have the promotional money to go after everyone at once, he went after this new market first. It was time for the first of the Pepsi Generation, for a drink to be consumed by "those who think young." It was a drink for the suburbs; it was a drink for its time.

And it was not a good time for Coca-Cola. Archie Lee had died in 1950. An attempt to make a run on the Pepsi constituency, the young sophisticate market, resulted in a series of magazine ads showing upwardly mobile young adults in what were taken to be exotic, expensive locations—hotels at Cannes, resorts in Acapulco, and the like. If, one day, Mrs. Pat Nixon appeared, with a Sassoon haircut, granny glasses, with no bra above and hot pants below, and if—remember, this is all fantasy—she looked *terrific*, still, she wouldn't look terrific. Because people would be doing double-takes and double-double-takes; it is a rule of fashion that you cannot look terrific if people gape at you.

D'Arcy began to flounder, replacing the paintings in the ads with color photography. But some mysterious *something* (and this went for *all* color advertising photography of the period that appeared in magazines), either in the state of the art or in women's makeups or printing techniques, made photographs of people, but women especially, look like photographs of overripe oranges. Compounding this misery, the ads for Coke were arranged in postwar modern—quasi-Mondrianesque boxes. In 1955 The Coca-Cola Company severed its 49-year relationship with D'Arcy, and hired a new advertising agency, McCann-Erickson. McCann promptly spent $250,000 experimenting with color photography, finding that whatever the difficulty with photographing people, there was no problem whatever in photographing food. The results of the experiments began to appear in luncheonettes and magazines of the '60s— glorious, drool-inducing photos of BLT sandwiches or thick wedges of steamy pizza, flanked by frosted bottles or glasses of Coca-Cola. (The owner of a photographic studio in Atlanta, who rents out his space and equipment to the hired guns from McCann when they come down from New York, reports that a single shot of a glass of Coca-Cola, suitably beaded with sweat, usually takes a full day to capture on film: art imitates life, but slowly.)

Even with McCann's work, it was not a good time for Coca-Cola. Steele had introduced new sizes for Pepsi, smaller bottles, which could be used in vending machines. The bottlers of Coke were screaming for new sizes, and new soft drinks to boot, the better to defend themselves against an onslaught of new, citrus-flavored drinks. In advertising terms, Coke had been outpositioned. The "light" cola in tune with modern tastes was supposed to be Pepsi. Soft drinks other than cola were more in keeping with all those slim, beautiful young people.) Slowly, almost painfully, Atlanta abandoned its single-product, single-container policy. The Company introduced the Fanta line and diet drinks and Coke itself was introduced in 12-ounce bottles, then cans, then no-deposit bottles. (The first no-deposit bottles were straight-sided, stumpy, and particularly ugly, looking like nothing so much as bottles of some cheapo brand of beer. The Los Angeles bottler refused to use them, demanding that Atlanta supply a model for a hobble-skirt no-deposit bottle. Atlanta did, looked at the results, and decided that what was good for Los Angeles was good for the rest of the country.)

The major soft drink companies found themselves faced with another marketing problem in the new America. After the second world war, Americans became an oddly mobile people — mobile in the sense that they traveled, yes, but that they traveled in private cars, which removed their trips from the discipline of train, plane, and bus schedules (ah, freedom!), but subjected them to the vagaries of road conditions and weather. Prior to the '60s, prudent travelers in cars loaded up before-hand with auto club route maps and lodging guides. Around two in the afternoon, estimates were made as to how long everyone could keep going, and then calls were placed to motels, not only for the simple security of having a room waiting, but to protect against having to stay the night in some . . . unsuitable . . . room. The American fear of the unknown in food and lodging (reinforced by tales of epic diarrhea in foreign countries, the memory of shack-like motels of the '30s, and the Bates Motel in *Psycho*) left precious few things to be sure of; among these were nationally known soft drinks.

Other corporations noted this fear, and where Quality Courts used to be only a rating organization, conferring its seal on motels meeting certain high standards, it later became an innkeeper along the lines of Holiday Inns. Chains like Howard Johnson's spread across the country, and began serving their own brand of cola. More profit for Mr. Johnson, and the turnpike traveler would swallow his desire for a Coke or Pepsi or Seven-Up and accept the HoJo Cola because that was the only thing available to wash down the Hojo hotdog.

The private label concept spread to large supermarket chains. Valuable shelf space in the area marked soft drinks was given over to brands belonging to the market. At many Safeway markets, for example, Cragmont pop would be given a huge amount of shelf area, with the major stacks of Coke and Pepsi placed adjacent to (and sometimes not so adjacent to) the area where a consumer would expect to find all soda pop. Vending machines in such stores would, naturally, carry the house brand, too. The consumer was rewarded, of course, with lower prices for the house brands. The major soft drink companies were rewarded with an erosion of their authority in the marketplace. So the taste of the home brands was different. But was it *worse,* or so noticeably *worse* that the consumer would pay more for the originals? We all know what the answer would be in the corporate headquarters for Coke or Pepsi. But the soft drink companies were in no position to demand that the stores pull house brands off the shelves. Like other national food manufacturers, they only could hope that their advertising and promotional power would persuade the customer to buy their product.

Unlike other food manufacturers, however, soft drink companies had, by the '60s, begun, seemingly of their own free will, to begin to erode their own primary authority in their field. Whatever myths were built into the act of drinking one brand of soft drink or another, they all were rationalized by the consumer as a matter of *taste.* Very few devotees of Pepsi, for example, would argue their preference by saying that drinking Pepsi put them into a different sociological or socio-economic class than consumers of Coke or Royal Crown. But they very well *might* say, "Pepsi *tastes* lighter."

The key word there, of course, is *tastes.* It was only through taste that the consumer could justify a choice which in fact might have been made for a number of reasons predicated by acceptance of advertising or promotion. Naturally, you might assume that no soft drink manufacturer would mess around in the area of taste, right? Wrong.

Pepsi was busily being sold to young (or younger) beautiful people, who are not, by and large, supposed to be fat.

Clearly, drinking a beverage that is primarily made up of sugar and water is not the same as snacking on one Ry-Krisp and a half a grapefruit, but Pepsi was supposed to be "lighter" than Coke. (For a time, Pepsi did have less sugar-per-ounce, until the sugar content of Coke was reduced.) Whatever difficulty this marketing scheme was causing The Coca-Cola Company, and it was considerable, it was even more of a problem for the Royal Crown Company. Royal Crown operated out of a home base of Columbus, Georgia, a city renowned only for its proximity to Fort Benning. Royal Crown was to Coke what Columbus was to Atlanta. Worse than that, the formulation of Royal Crown was such that only a very well-developed palate could distinguish it from Pepsi. Royal Crown came in 12-ounce bottles. Royal Crown, therefore, was getting murdered by Pepsi.

Well, if Pepsi was appealing to young sophisticates, and if the Pepsi generation was so damned good-looking, and if people were having difficulty with the simple problem of gluttony, then why not introduce an out-and-out diet cola? Which The Royal Crown Company did around 1960: Diet-Rite. It was an immediate success. (Pepsi quickly brought out a diet drink called Patio Cola, which fizzed out, since the name did not strike consumers as being diet-oriented.) By the third quarter of 1961, diet drinks had captured an astounding 16.1 percent of the entire soft drink market. Even with this obvious market penetration, The Coca-Cola Company held off introducing Tab until 1963, and then did so after considerable internal debate.

For the real question to be resolved in the matter of diet drinks was in the matter of taste. You did not have to be a research chemist at the Food and Drug Administration or at a soft drink company to know one thing about artificial sweetners: they cause diet drinks to taste somewhat metallic and leave a noticable aftertaste in the mouth. (The Seven-Up Company wound up playing against this very fact in its advertising for Diet 7UP: "A diet drink that doesn't taste funny.")

The first formulations used saccharine, which *really* tasted funny. Then, of course, some wizard discovered cyclamates, which tasted slightly less bad. Sales, which had been sliding off (no more of the fitness and vigor of the Kennedy years, for one thing), again hit 16.1 percent of the market in the second quarter of 1968.

In November of that year, of course, the bad news about cyclamates was announced, and sales plummeted as manufacturers raced to substitute saccharine and/or small amounts of sugar in their formulae. Sales bottomed out at 9.3 percent of the market in December, 1970.

Retrospectively, one can argue that, given the generally slapdash methods of the FDA, the manufacturers themselves should have been leery of cyclamates (and saccharine, too, for that matter). But the promotion of diet drinks by the two leaders in soft drinks chipped away at the concept of the inviolability of taste of their major products. Very few major dairies, by way of comparison, are aggressively in the margarine business, primarily because they recognize that what they are selling with butter is the *taste* of butter.

An overweight consumer of soft drinks could very well explain his purchase of a diet drink with the frank admission that he was putting up with the taste in order to lose weight, but in actively promoting such substitutions, the major soft drink manufacturers were conditioning the public to accept an inferior taste. If the public could learn to accept *that,* it could certainly accept the different taste of a private label drink.

As The Coca-Cola Company grappled with its merchandising, its ad agency, McCann, was trying to come to grips with television, which was in the process of becoming what it is today: the mass-market medium, replacing the general interest magazine. In its earliest days, TV ads were restricted by the very live-ness of the medium: a hot number was Arthur Godfrey holding up a can of something and delivering a spiel for it; what that was, was radio with pictures. The coaxial cable, better quality film, and finally videotape, changed the rules. But if it freed ads from the tyranny of the live performance, that very technology ushered in an age of dumb in the programming of TV. Finally, some smart ad men realized that the extraordinary rottenness of TV—that is, the sneering condescension on the part of TV executives in New York and Hollywood, which allowed them to shovel steaming piles of crap at the American people as the logical alternative to the turgid junk which those same moguls took to be Culture—made a perfect setting for terrific advertising. Terrific advertising, in this case, is defined as a commercial upon which is lavished that wit, expertise, and intelligence which you suppose should be the basic component parts of any self-respecting TV program.

Even if the theory of the brilliant commercial was acceptable for Coke or Pepsi, in practice it was difficult to construct, because commercials have traditionally been thought of as little stories. A thirty-second *War and Peace*. A one-minute *Guys and Dolls*. This worked for a lot of products, spectacularly so with the new commitment to excellence (Alka-Seltzer, for one), but it wasn't so hot for soft drinks. What is the soft drink story, anyway? Buying it and getting it home are not such snappy numbers, which leaves *drinking* it. Well, drinking soda pop, like making love, is an extremely pleasurable (or at its worst, a pleasantly pleasurable) experience which in large part resists being captured on film. Explicit love-making, when shown on film for more than 30 seconds, always resembles the cinematic equivalent of *Mechanix Illustrated*. Anything over five seconds of any one person drinking soda pop is slightly less interesting than that.

The solution, for Coke and Pepsi, came out of the work of film-makers like Richard Lester, whose quick-cutting techniques pointed the way to commercials which didn't have to tell a linear story at all. By using a mosaic of film snippets, TV commercials could show the face of America in much the same way that Archie Lee's magazine ads had shown the face of America. Snap. A black Cub Scout holding a Pepsi. Snap. Bicycle riders pedalling through a forest in a Coke commercial. Snap. A boy and girl resting easily in a meadow. Snap. Snap. Snap.

These commercials came at a perfect time, since they saved both Pepsi and Coke from being products labelled as anti-feminist. Aside from the fact that no soft drink commercial had ever portrayed women as the helpless, witless creatures who inhabit the world of floor wax, vitamin and margarine users (to name just a few products that use women in a degrading manner), the quick-cut technique, with its diversity of faces, races, and ages, could not and did not use the woman as sex object.

As good as this advertising was, it was not half as provocative (perhaps because it didn't have to be) as that of 7-Up. The major marketing difficulty of 7-Up (or 7UP, as it now likes to be known) was that it wasn't a cola, a discovery akin to a man realizing

172.

that the reason he isn't everything that Cary Grant is, is that he isn't Cary Grant. If 7UP wasn't a cola, it wasn't a cola, and it decided to attack the problem head on, labelling itself the Uncola, and mixing nutty, inventive TV commercials (some in the "Yellow Submarine" cartoon style, others using whimsy or satire) with super-graphic billboards. (Dr. Pepper, which was just beginning to crack the major metropolitan markets of New York and Los Angeles in the late '60s and early '70s, also used a merchandising and advertising campaign that played against itself. Ads in newspapers explained the history of the drink, and said that the name Dr. Pepper did not mean that the beverage was medicinal. By 1973 Dr. Pepper was the fourth largest-selling soft drink, behind Coke, Pepsi, and 7UP; it just edged out RC, which was being sold in giant 16-ounce bottles—more for your money, to be sure, but often more than you wanted to drink—and advertised as being "light in sugar and light in gas.")

The advertising for 7UP had the added advantage of being perfect for the "youth market," that is the youth market as it was defined after rock and roll got chic in 1965. That was a sensitive area for both Coca-Cola and Pepsi because of the obvious relationship between that world and drugs. On the West Coast, a shrewd young entrepreneur hired a commercial artist to write out the word "cocaine" in script reminiscent of the mark for Coca-Cola for use in a poster. It was quickly picked up by other merchants and put on T-shirts. This was not considered in the least bit humorous in Atlanta.

Pepsico had its share of problems, too. In 1967, a contract was signed putting ads for Pepsi on the back cover of a new slick magazine (Cheetah) aimed at the youth market. Naturally, the magazine published articles about drugs. Naturally, someone got hold of a copy, circled the references to drugs and the four-letter words, and sent it to an executive of Pepsico. Naturally, Pepsico decided to cancel its advertising. Since the ads had originally been placed in part because Pepsi was served at Cheetah discotheques, a representative of the magazine had a meeting to discuss the cancellation, not with the ad agency, but with an executive of Pepsico. The Pepsico exec explained the company's position . . . horrible, shocking, impossible. The representative of the magazine pointed out that the offensive story had been a reportage account of the smuggling of marijuana from Tijuana to Los Angeles, and certainly hadn't endorsed either smuggling or marijuana, nor the smuggler's language. That didn't matter, was the answer. People who were interested in marijuana were not the sort that Pepsi should be associated with. With the game lost, the magazine rep pulled out all the stops. Be realistic, he said. What if *every* reader of the magazine is a marijuana smoker? Do you know what *happens* to a person high on marijuana? He gets incredibly *thirsty*. And a person thirsty from marijuana is a *person who will drink a lot of Pepsi-Cola*. At that, the man from Pepsico turned pale and rushed out of the room.

Later, of course, McCann found an easy and shrewd way into the youth market for Coke when it hired a bunch of topflight rock performers and had each of them sing the current jingle for Coke in the performer's own style, for radio air-play. Then McCann went one step further, and commissioned its own socko hit record, *It's the Real Thing* (a slogan, by the way, which had first been used for Coke in 1941).

POP.

CHAPTER 15

We have been talking about a vision of ourselves as projected or reflected by the advertising of, for the most part, one company. Since that company makes a lot of money and spends a lot of money, it is fair to close by noting that it has greater responsibilities than holding a mirror up to us in such a way that we will see ourselves and not incidentally be moved to drink some pop.

For all the money it has spent and is spending to get us to drink its products, the single most curious thing about The Coca-Cola Company is the money it doesn't spend promoting its corporate self. Over the past few years, The Coca-Cola Company as well as Pepsico, have drawn amazing amounts of criticism for various company activities. The no-deposit bottle, brilliant idea that it was once thought to be, is now recognized as an ecological bomb, and both major soft drink companies are trying to find containers which will self-destruct. Executives will say privately that they and their bottlers would be more than happy to go back to deposit bottles, since deposit bottles are cheaper. But no one firm can stop using no-deposits unilaterally for fear of losing entirely the lazy soft drink drinker.

In 1970, some months after the president of the Coca-Cola Company had announced (internally) a program to upgrade the living standards of farm workers who work at the Company's Minute Maid subsidiary, a TV network news show delivered of itself an hour on the shameful plight of the farm worker, zeroing in, of course, on the Minute Maid operation, yet neglecting to mention the money that was in the process of being poured into that operation for the workers. It was a dark moment in Atlanta, and yet, in all the time since then, the Company has never bought space or air-time to show the work it has done, the standards it has set, for the workers at Minute Maid. It may be that someone at the Atlanta headquarters has looked at ads showing clean rivers (placed by corporations whose spewing plants are *downstream* of the area photographed), decided that all of us suspect large corporations of bending the truth into a pretzel on their own behalfs, and said, the hell with it, we'll spend our energies doing what we should be doing, not boasting about it.

If that be the case, then let this be the record that, as Pepsico was fleeing the problems of the big city (New York) for the sweet dreams of suburban life, establishing its corporate headquarters in Rye, New York, The Coca-Cola Company was plunking its new headquarters building right next to the tracks which divide the right side of Atlanta from the wrong (read black) one. That's an expensive way of saying that the Company has a stake in the city. But if they'd *only* built the damn thing in the shape of a Coca-Cola bottle. . . .

With Pepsi now licensed for sale in the Soviet Union, and Pepsico operating in fields far removed from soft drinks (truck rentals, for one), and with The Coca-Cola Company selling coffee and other products, it is clear that the corporate thrust of the soft drink industry is toward the sort of expansion that has marked the recent history of American business. Obviously, trying to predict the future growth of these companies (will they buy California wineries? Nathan's Hot Dogs? The Dixie Cup Company?) is impossible.

But if the special sin of big business is big arrogance (what is good for ITT is good for the world), it is perhaps a cause for optimism that the financial foundation for the soft drink manufacturer is the consumption of a product so trivial that few men can inflate the intrinsic worth of the product itself.

Soda pop will not save the world. And that is probably a good thing.

POP.

APPENDIX

Any book that wants to be taken seriously—a footnote to history!—should have an appendix, and this book shall be no exception.

For all of the energy expended in protecting the secrecy of the formulas of Coke and Pepsi, and for all of the energy and money expended making you think that you are getting the exact same drink wherever you go in the world, the plain truth is that, secret though the formulas are, they are not sacrosanct.

Put bluntly, the formula for Pepsi is changed to accommodate the apparent taste preference in at least one part of the country—the South. A bottle of Pepsi purchased in the deep South tastes like, well, it tastes like—well, it's *supposed* to taste like Coke.

This matter was brought up to an executive of The Coca-Cola Company, who was asked if the formula for Coke was modified in any part of the country to conform to regional tastes. Coke, he replied, may taste different in different parts of the country because of the difference in the water available there.

Finally, worth the price of any appendix, for cola aficionados who want to taste the best of the colas, the best bottles of Pepsi available in the United States are in Hawaii (10 oz.). Coke is also superb in Hawaii (try the Coke bottled by the Kauai Soda Co., on the island of Kauai), but the best Coke in the U.S. is—can't you guess?—dispensed through the premix founts in the headquarters of The Coca-Cola Company in Atlanta.

ACKNOWLEDGEMENTS

Obviously, a lot of people were of great help in getting this book together. Tauni and Mike Brustin of Los Angeles were gracious enough to lend me much of their massive collection of artifacts so that they could be photographed. The photography was done by Mike Salisbury, John Paul Endress, Marvin Mitchell, and Harold Terhune in Atlanta, and Marty Evans in Los Angeles. Many rare transparencies and black-and-white photos are from the files of Harald J. Torgeson, who had an incredible collection of business antiques until he sold out to become Director of The Ships of the Sea Maritime Museum in Savannah, Georgia.

Tom Mitchell, a vice president of the D'Arcy Advertising Agency, was helpful in making D'Arcy's files available and arranging interviews with artists. I am indebted to Laney Lee for sharing his memories of his father. Jim Ball of Dr. Pepper provided graphics and a history of his company.

Dennis Borgman of 7-Up went out of his way to furnish some rare transparencies of that company's early advertising. Of course, the bulk of the material in the book—even some about competitors—came from The Coca-Cola Company. Bill Pruett, Bill Bass, and Ken Manson were unfailingly unflappable while I pestered them with outrageous demands. Julius Lunsford, Jr. cleared up some questions about complicated legal battles The Coca-Cola Company has been involved in over the years.

One man, however, should get major credit for the existence of this book. Wilbur G. Kurtz, Jr., Archives Director of The Coca-Cola Company, has doggedly, over the years, compiled material pertaining to the history of Coke. Without these materials and his unstinting efforts in making them available to me, this book could never have been written. I would also like to thank his secretary, Mrs. Margaret Hopper, who not only dug out the things I needed, but kept me from sinking face-down into the piles of research by dousing me with an endless supply of ice-cold Coca-Cola.

The least celebrated friend and ally of a writer generally is his agent, who serves as psychoanalyst, and when a writer's book doesn't do as well as *The Carpetbaggers,* whipping boy. It has been a great pleasure for me to have been represented by Don Gold, the most decent and kind person I have met in the communications business. The various negotiations for this book were also entered into on my behalf by Tom Pollock, a nifty young lawyer in L.A. His legal expertise and encouragement made the epic quality of his bills somewhat easier reading. I should also note that the actual editing of the manuscript was done with great skill and tact by Ms. Jamie Shalleck.

Finally, the patience and occasional impatience of Marianne Partridge made the writing of this book a little less impossible.